Rick S

SNAPSHOT

D0901468

Basque
Country
Spain & France

CONTENTS

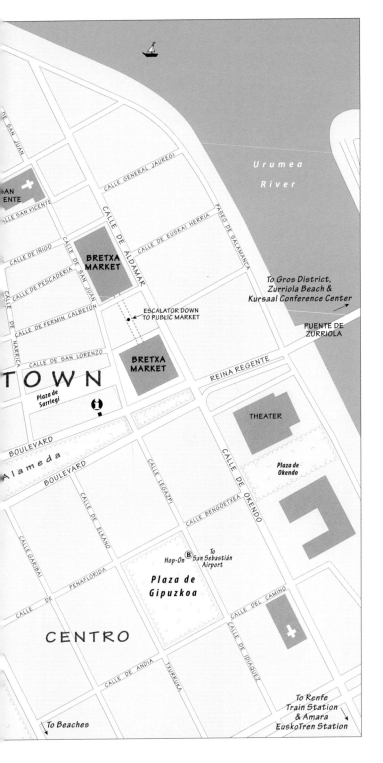

Urumea
River

DE SAN JUAN

CALLE GENERAL JAUREGI

CALLE SAN VICENTE

SAN
ENTE

CALLE DE ALDAMAR

CALLE DE EUSKAI HERRIA

PASEO DE SALAMANCA

CALLE DE INIGO

BRETXA
MARKET

CALLE DE PESCADERIA

CALLE DE SAN JUAN

CALLE DE

CALLE DE FERMIN CALBETON

To Gros District,
Zurriola Beach &
Kursaal Conference Center

NARRICA

ESCALATOR DOWN
TO PUBLIC MARKET

PUENTE DE
ZURRIOLA

CALLE DE SAN LORENZO

BRETXA
MARKET

T O W N

REINA REGENTE

Plaza de
Sarriegi

THEATER

CALLE DE OKENDO

Plaza de
Okendo

BOULEVARD

Alameda

BOULEVARD

CALLE LEGAZPI

CALLE PENGOETXEA

CALLE DE ELKANO

CALLE GARIBAI

CALLE DE

PENAFLORIDA

Hop-On Ⓑ San Sebastián
Airport

To
San Sebastián
Airport

Plaza de
Gipuzkoa

CALLE DEL CAMINO

CENTRO

CALLE DE IDIAQUEZ

CALLE DE ANDIA

TXURRUKA

To Beaches

To Renfe
Train Station
& Amara
EuskoTren Station

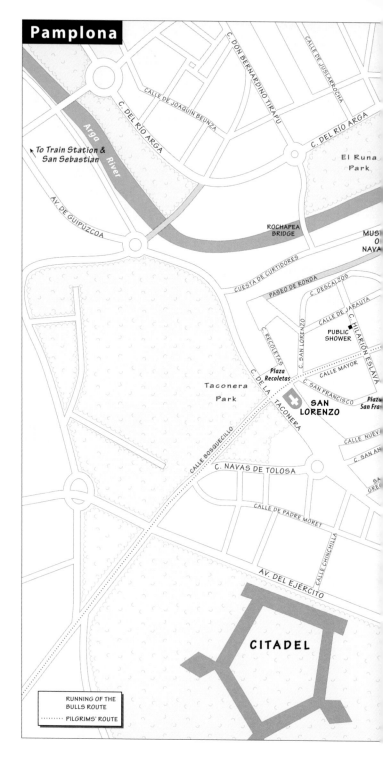

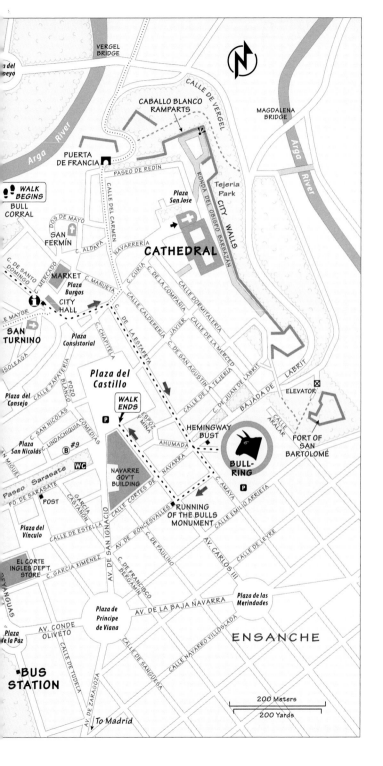

INTRODUCTION

This Snapshot guide, excerpted from my guidebook on Spain, introduces you to the Basque Country. This is the land where Spain and France meet the Atlantic--filled with people who have their own culture and language, but not their own country. Even without political independence, the Basque culture thrives in both countries. Here you can enjoy the cushy beach resorts of San Sebastián and Biarritz, just as European royalty did a hundred years ago. Or make a pilgrimage to the historic town of Guernica, where horrific bombing during the Spanish Civil War inspired a Picasso masterpiece. Visit Bilbao and Frank Gehry's dazzling temple of modern art--the Guggenheim Bilbao. Run with (or cheer on) the bulls in Pamplona. Across the border in France, linger in Bayonne, with its lively old town and impressive Museum of Basque Culture, and then head for the mellow port town of St-Jean-de-Luz. In the village of St-Jean-Pied-de-Port, watch pilgrims begin their Camino journey in the foothills of the Pyrenees. On both sides of the border, you'll see why the independent Basques have clung tightly to their heritage.

To help you have the best trip possible, I've included the following topics in this book:

· **Planning Your Time,** with advice on how to make the most of your limited time

· **Orientation,** including tourist information offices (abbreviated as TI), tips on public transportation, local tour options, and helpful hints

· **Sights,** with ratings and strategies for meaningful and efficient visits

· **Sleeping** and **Eating,** with good-value recommendations in every price range

· **Connections,** with tips on trains, buses, and driving

Practicalities, near the end of this book, has information on money, staying connected, hotel reservations, transportation, and other helpful hints, plus Spanish and French survival phrases.

To travel smartly, read this little book in its entirety before you go. It's my hope that this guide will make your trip more meaningful and rewarding. Traveling like a temporary local, you'll get the absolute most out of every mile, minute, and dollar.

Buen viaje and *bon voyage!* Happy travels!

Rick Steves

BASQUE COUNTRY

Euskal Herria

Straddling two nations on the Atlantic Coast—stretching about 100 miles from Bilbao, Spain north to Bayonne, France—lies the ancient, free-spirited land of the Basques. The Basque Country is famous for its beaches, culinary scene, and scintillating modern architecture...and for its feisty, industrious natives. It's also simply beautiful: Bold stone houses and bright white chalet-style homes with deep-red and green shutters scatter across lush, rolling hills; the Pyrenees Mountains soar high above the Atlantic; and surfers and sardines share the waves.

Insulated from mainstream Europe for much of their history, the plucky Basques have wanted to be left alone for more than 7,000 years. An easily crossed border separates the French *Pays Basque* from the Spanish *País Vasco,* allowing you to sample both sides from a single base (in Spain, I prefer fun-loving San Sebastián; in France, I hang my beret in cozy St-Jean-de-Luz).

Much unites the Spanish and French Basque regions: They share a cuisine, Union Jack-style flag (green, red, and white), and common language (Euskara), spoken by about a half-million people. (Virtually everyone also speaks Spanish and/or French.) And both have been integrated by their respective nations, sometimes forcibly. The French Revolution quelled French Basque ideas of independence; 130 years later, Spain's fascist dictator, Generalísimo Francisco Franco, attempted to tame his own separatist-minded Basques.

But over the past few generations, things have started looking up. The long-suppressed Euskara language is enjoying a resurgence. And, as the European Union celebrates ethnic regions rather than nations, the Spanish and French Basques are feeling more united.

Basque Country at a Glance

▲▲**San Sebastián (Spain)** Relaxing upscale city with beachfront promenade wrapped around chic shopping neighborhood and tasty tapas bars.

▲▲**Bilbao (Spain)** Revitalized regional capital with architectural gem—Guggenheim Bilbao—and atmospheric old town.

▲▲**St-Jean-de-Luz (France)** Sleepy seaside retreat in the French *Pays Basque* that serves as home base for countryside exploration.

▲**Guernica (Spain)** Village at the heart of Basque culture that was devastated by bombs during the Spanish Civil War—later immortalized by a Picasso masterpiece.

▲**Bayonne (France)** Urban French scene with a Basque twist, home to impressive cultural museum, scenic ramparts, and lots of ham.

Biarritz (France) Beach resort known for its mix of international glitz and surfer dudes.

▲▲**Pamplona (Spain)** Thriving Basque town with atmospheric narrow lanes, fine churches, and world-famous Running of the Bulls.

▲**St-Jean-Pied-de-Port (France)** Tranquil mountain village clustered along a babbling stream—the perfect springboard for the Camino de Santiago.

This heavily industrialized region is enjoying a striking 21st-century renaissance. In Spain, the dazzling architecture of the Guggenheim Bilbao modern-art museum and the glittering resort of San Sebastián are drawing enthusiastic crowds. And, in France, long-ignored cities such as Bayonne and the surfing mecca of Biarritz are being revitalized. At the same time, traditional small towns—like Spain's Lekeitio and France's St-Jean-de-Luz and nearby mountain villages—are also thriving, making the entire region colorful, fun, welcoming...and unmistakably Basque.

PLANNING YOUR TIME

One day is enough for a quick sample of the Basque Country, but two or three days lets you breathe deep and hold it in. Where you go depends on your interests: Spain or France? Cities (such as Bilbao and Bayonne) or resorts (such as San Sebastián and St-Jean-de-Luz)?

If you want to slow down and focus on Spain, spend one day

relaxing in San Sebastián and the second side-tripping to Bilbao (and Guernica, if you have a car).

Better yet, take this easy opportunity to dip into France. Sleep in one country, then side-trip into the other, devoting one day to Spain (either San Sebastián or Bilbao), and a second day to France (St-Jean-de-Luz and Bayonne).

Wherever you go, your Basque sightseeing should be a fun blend of urban, rural, cultural, and culinary activities.

GETTING AROUND THE BASQUE COUNTRY

The tourist's Basque Country—from Bilbao to Bayonne—stays close to the coastline. Everything is connected by good roads and public transportation. If traveling between Spain and France, carry your passport, as police might ask for identification at border crossings.

By Bus and Train: From San Sebastián, the bus is the best way to reach Bilbao (and from there, bus or train to Guernica). To go between San Sebastián and France, you have a choice of train or bus. Trains offer more frequent departure times but require a transfer in Hendaye; buses can sometimes be faster and more convenient (check schedules and compare). Once in France, the three main towns—St-Jean-de-Luz, Bayonne, and Biarritz—are connected by bus and by train (and Bayonne and Biarritz by the electric Tram'bus). Even if you rent a car, I'd do these three towns by public transit due to the insane traffic during high season. Specific connections are explained in each section.

Note that a few out-of-the-way areas—Spain's Bay of Biscay and France's Basque villages of the interior—are impractical by public transportation...but worth the trouble by car.

By Car: San Sebastián, Bilbao, St-Jean-de-Luz, and Bayonne are connected by a convenient expressway, called AP-8 in Spain and A-63 in France (rough timings: Bilbao to San Sebastián, 1.5 hours; San Sebastián to St-Jean-de-Luz, 45 minutes; St-Jean-de-Luz to Bayonne, 30 minutes).

Language on Road Signs: At the start of each section, I list place names using the Spanish or French spelling first and the Euskara spelling second; throughout the rest of the chapter, I default to the spelling that prevails locally. While most people refer to towns by their Spanish or French names, many road signs list places in Euskara. (In Spain, signs are usually posted in both Euskara and Spanish, either on the same sign or with dual signage on opposite sides of the street. In less separatist-minded France, signs are often only in French.) The Spanish or French version is sometimes scratched out by locals, so you might have to navigate by Euskara names.

Also note that in terms of linguistic priority (e.g., museum information), Euskara comes first, Spanish and French tie for second, and English is a distant fourth...and it often doesn't make the cut.

BASQUE COUNTRY CUISINE SCENE

Mixing influences from the mountains, sea, Spain, and France, Basque food is reason enough to visit the region. The local cuisine—dominated by seafood, tomatoes, and red peppers—offers some spicy dishes, unusual in most of Europe. And though you'll find similar specialties throughout the Basque lands, Spain is still Spain and France is still France. Here are some dishes you're most likely to find in each area.

Spanish Basque Cuisine: Hopping from bar to bar sampling *pintxos*—the local term for tapas—is a highlight of any trip (for details, see the "Do the *Txikiteo*" sidebar, later). You'll want to try the famous *pil-pil*, made from emulsifying the skin of *bacalao* (dried, salted cod) into a mayonnaise-like sauce with chili and garlic. Another tasty dish is *kokotxas*, usually made from hake *(merluza)* fish cheeks, prepared like *pil-pil*, and cooked slowly over low heat so the natural gelatin is released, turning it into a wonderful sauce—*¡qué bueno!* Look also for white asparagus from Navarra. Wine-wise, I prefer the reds and rosés from Navarra. Local brews include *sidra* (hard apple cider) and *txakolí* (chah-koh-LEE, a light, sparkling white wine—often theatrically poured from high above the glass

for aeration). Wine-wise, I prefer the reds and rosés from Navarra. Finish your dinner with *cuajada,* a yogurt-like, creamy milk dessert that's sometimes served with honey and nuts. Another specialty, found throughout Spain, is *membrillo,* a sweet and *muy* dense quince jelly. Try it with cheese for a light dessert, or look for it at breakfast.

French Basque Cuisine: The red peppers (called *piments d'Espelette*) hanging from homes in small villages give foods a distinctive flavor and often end up in *piperade,* a dish that combines peppers, tomatoes, garlic, ham, and eggs. Peppers are also dried and used as condiments. Look for them with the terrific Basque dish *axoa* (a veal or lamb stew on mashed potatoes). Look also for anything "Basque-style" *(à la basquaise)*—cooked with tomato, eggplant, red pepper, and garlic. Don't leave without trying *ttoro* (tchoo-roh), a seafood stew that is the Basque Country's answer to bouillabaisse and cioppino. *Marmitako* is a hearty tuna stew. Local cheeses come from Pyrenean sheep's milk *(pur brebis),* and the local ham *(jambon de Bayonne)* is famous throughout France. After dinner try a shot of *izarra* (herbal-flavored brandy). To satisfy your sweet tooth, look for *gâteau basque,* a local tart filled with pastry cream or cherries from Bayonne. Hard apple cider is a tasty and

Who Are the Basques?

To call the Basques "mysterious" is an understatement. Before most European nations had ever set sail, Basque whalers competed with the Vikings for control of the sea. During the Industrial Revolution and lean Franco years, Basque steel kept the Spanish economy alive. In the last few decades, the separatist group ETA gave the Basque people an unwarranted reputation for violence. And through it all, the Basques have spoken a unique language that to outsiders sounds like gibberish or a secret code.

So just who are the Basques? Even for Basques, that's a difficult question. According to traditional stereotypes, Basques are thought of as having long noses, heavy eyebrows, floppy ears, stout bodies, and a penchant for wearing berets. But widespread Spanish and French immigration has made it difficult to know who actually has Basque ethnic roots. (In fact, some of the Basques' greatest patriots have had no Basque blood.) And so today, anyone who speaks the Basque language, Euskara, is considered a "Basque"—as are the many people who grew up under Franco and never had the chance to learn the language.

Euskara, related to no other surviving tongue, has been used since Neolithic times—making it, very likely, the oldest European language that's still spoken. With its seemingly impossible-to-pronounce words filled with k's, tx's, and z's (restrooms are *komunak: gizonak* for men and *emakumeak* for women), Euskara makes speaking Spanish suddenly seem easy. Try greeting locals with *kaixo* and saying goodbye with *agur.* (Some tips: *tx* is pronounced "ch" and *tz* is pronounced "ts." Other key words: *kalea* is "street," and *ostatua* is a cheap hotel.) Kept alive as a symbol of Basque cultural identity, Euskara typically is learned proudly as a second or third language. Many locals can switch effortlessly from Euskara to Spanish or French.

The Basque economy has historically been shaped by three factors: the sea, agriculture, and iron deposits.

Basque sailors were some of the first and finest in Europe, as they built ever-better boats to venture farther and farther into the Atlantic in search of whales and cod. By the mid-15th century, Basque sailors were venturing a thousand miles from home into the far northern Atlantic Ocean. Despite lack of physical evidence, many historians surmise that the Basques must have sailed to Newfoundland before Christopher Columbus landed in the Caribbean.

When the "Spanish" era of exploration began, Basques continued to play a key role, as sailors and shipbuilders. Columbus' *Santa María* was likely Basque built, and his crew included many

Basques. History books teach that Ferdinand Magellan was the first to circumnavigate the globe, with the footnote that he was killed partway around. Who took over the helm for the rest of the journey, completing the circle? It was his Basque captain, Juan Sebastián de Elcano. And a pair of well-traveled Catholic priests, known for their far-reaching missionary trips that led to founding the Jesuit order, were also Basques: St. Ignatius of Loyola and St. Francis Xavier.

Later, the Industrial Age swept Europe, gaining a foothold in Iberia when the Basques began using their rich iron deposits to make steel. Pioneering Basque industrialists set the tempo as they dragged Spain into the modern world. Cities such as Bilbao were heavily industrialized, sparking an influx of workers from around Spain (which gradually diluted Basque blood in the Basque Country).

The independence-minded Basques are notorious for their stubbornness. In truth, as a culturally and linguistically unique is-

land surrounded by bigger and stronger nations, the Basques have learned to compromise. Historically Basques have remained on good terms with outsiders, so long as their traditional laws, the *Fueros,* were respected. Though outdated, the *Fueros* continue to symbolize a self-governance that the Basques hold dear. It is only when foreign law has been placed above the *Fueros*—as many of today's Basques feel Spanish law is—that the people become agitated.

In recent years, much of the news of the Basques—especially in Spain—was made by the terrorist organization ETA, whose goal had been to establish an independent Basque state. (ETA stands for the Euskara phrase *"Euskadi Ta Askatasuna,"* or "Basque Country and Freedom.") ETA is thought to have been responsible for more than 800 deaths since 1968. The group gradually disarmed in recent years, and finally announced its dissolution in April 2018, with apologies to victims and their families.

This is only a first glimpse into the important, quirky, and fascinating Basque people. To better understand the Basques, there's no better book than Mark Kurlansky's *The Basque History of the World*—essential pretrip reading for historians. And various museums in this region also illuminate Basque culture and history, including the Museum of San Telmo in San Sebastián, the Assembly House and Basque Country Museum in Guernica, and the Museum of Basque Culture in Bayonne (all described in this book).

local beverage. The regional wine Irouléguy comes in red, white, and rosé, and is the only wine produced in the French part of Basque Country (locals like to say that it's made from the smallest vineyard in France but the biggest in the Northern Basque Country).

Spanish Basque Country

Four of the seven Basque territories lie within Spain, where they're known as El País Vasco. Many consider Spanish Basque culture to be feistier and more colorful than the relatively assimilated French Basques—you'll hear more Euskara spoken here than in France.

For nearly 40 years, beginning in 1939, the figure of Generalísimo Franco loomed large over the Spanish Basques. Franco depended upon Basque industry to keep the floundering Spanish economy afloat. But even as he exploited the Basques economically, he so effectively blunted their culture that the language was primarily Spanish by default. Franco kicked off his regime by offering up the historic Basque town of Guernica as target practice to Hitler's air force. The notorious result—the wholesale slaughter of innocent civilians—was immortalized by Pablo Picasso's mural *Guernica.*

But Franco is long gone, and today's Basques are looking to the future. The iron deposits have been depleted, prompting the Basques to reimagine their rusting cities for the 21st century. True to form, they're rising to the challenge. Perhaps the best example is Bilbao, whose iconic Guggenheim Museum—built on the former site of an industrial wasteland—is the centerpiece of a bold new skyline.

San Sebastián is the heart of the tourist's País Vasco, with its sparkling, picturesque beach framed by looming green mountains and a charming old town with gourmet *pintxos* (tapas) spilling out of every bar. On-the-rise Bilbao is worth a look for its landmark Guggenheim and its atmospheric old town. For small-town fun, drop by the fishing village of Lekeitio (near Bilbao). And for history, Guernica has some intriguing museums.

San Sebastián / Donostia

Shimmering above the breathtaking Concha Bay, elegant and prosperous San Sebastián (Donostia in Euskara, which locals lovingly shorten to Donosti) has a favored location, with golden beaches capped by twin peaks at either end and a cute little island offshore. A delightful beachfront promenade runs the length of the bay, with a charismatic old town at one end and a smart shopping district in the center. It has 186,000 residents and almost that many tourists in high season (July-Sept). With a romantic setting, a soaring statue of Christ gazing over the city, and a late-night lively old town, San Sebastián has a mini Rio de Janeiro aura. Though the actual "sightseeing" isn't much, the scenic city itself provides a pleasant introduction to Spain's Basque Country. As a culinary capital of

Spain—with many local restaurants getting international attention—competition is tight to dish up some of the top tapas anywhere.

In 1845, Queen Isabel II's doctor recommended she treat her skin problems by bathing here in the sea. (For modesty's sake, she would go inside a giant cabana that could be wheeled into the surf—allowing her to swim far from prying eyes, never having to set foot on the beach.) Her visit mobilized Spain's aristocracy, and soon the city was on the map as a seaside resort. By the turn of the 20th century, San Sebastián was the toast of the belle époque, and a leading resort for Europe's beautiful people. Before World War I, Queen María Cristina summered here and held court in her Miramar Palace overlooking the crescent beach (the turreted, red-brick building partway around the bay). Hotels, casinos, and theaters flourished. Even Franco enjoyed 35 summers in a place he was sure to call San Sebastián, not Donostia.

PLANNING YOUR TIME

San Sebastián's sights can be exhausted in a few hours, but it's a great place to be on vacation for a full, lazy day (or longer). Stroll the two-mile-long promenade with the locals and scout the place you'll grab to work on a tan. The promenade leads to a funicular that lifts you to the Monte Igueldo viewpoint, unless you're up for hiking to the top. After exploring the old town and port, walk up to the hill of Monte Urgull. If you have more time, enjoy the delightful aquarium or the free history museum inside Monte Urgull's old castle. Or check out the Museum of San Telmo, the largest of its kind on Basque culture, which tracks the evolution of this unique society with state-of-the-art displays. A key ingredient of any visit to San Sebastián is enjoying tapas *(pintxos)* in the old-town bars.

Orientation to San Sebastián

The San Sebastián that we're interested in surrounds Concha Bay (Bahía de la Concha). It can be divided into three areas: Playa de la Concha (best beaches), Centro (the shopping district), and the old town (the skinny, grid-planned streets north of Centro called Parte Vieja). Centro, just east of Playa de la Concha, has beautiful turn-of-the-20th-century architecture, but no real sights. A busy drag called the Boulevard stands where the city

wall once ran, and separates the Centro from the old town.

It's all bookended by small mountains: Monte Urgull on the east end of the bay, and Monte Igueldo to the west. The river (Río Urumea) divides central San Sebastián from the district called Gros, with a lively night scene and surfing beach.

TOURIST INFORMATION

There are two **city-oriented TIs** in San Sebastián: on the Boulevard (Mon-Sat 9:00-20:00, off-season until 19:00; Sun 10:00-19:00, off-season until 14:00; Boulevard 8) and next to the Renfe train station (Mon-Sat 9:00-18:00, Sun 10:00-14:00, 22 Frantzia Pasealekua). The TIs share contact information (+34 943-481-166, www.sansebastianturismo.eus). The larger Boulevard TI has a touch screen outside that you can use to get a map. Both TIs offer handy pamphlets with self-guided walking tours—the Old Town/Monte Urgull walk is best—as well as guided walking tours (see "Tours in San Sebastián," later).

A **regional TI,** on the Boulevard next to the city TI at #6, focuses on the Gipuzkoa region in which San Sebastián sits (daily 10:00-14:00 & 15:30-20:00, may have shorter Sun hours off-season, +34 943 415 151, www.sansebastianregion.com).

Sightseeing Cards: The **San Sebastián Card** gives you small discounts for some restaurants, museums, and stores, half price on one of the TI's guided tours, and includes a number of rides on public transportation (€9 for 6 rides, €16 for 12 rides; shareable with one other person). It's not worth the cost unless you expect to ride public transit a lot—and the city is small enough that you probably won't. If you're exploring the larger region, the TI also sells the **Basque Card,** but for most travelers it's also not worth it.

ARRIVAL IN SAN SEBASTIÁN

By Train: The town has two train stations (neither has baggage storage, but you can leave bags nearby—see "Helpful Hints," later).

If you're coming on a regional train from Hendaye/Hendaia on the French border, get off at the **Amara EuskoTren station** (five stops before the end of the line, which is called Lasarte-Oria). It's a level 15-minute walk to the center: Exit the station and walk across the long plaza, then veer right and walk eight blocks down Calle Easo (toward the statue of Christ hovering on the hill) to the beach. The old town will be ahead on your right, with Playa de la Concha to your left. To speed things up, exit the station to the right, catch bus #21, #26, or #28 along Calle Easo, and take it to the Boulevard stop, near the TIs at the bottom of the old town.

If you're arriving by train from elsewhere in Spain (or from France after transferring in Irún), you'll get off at the main **Renfe station.** It's just across the river from the Centro shopping district. To get to the old town, catch bus #9 from the city side of the station to the Boulevard stop (€1.80, pay driver) or catch a taxi (they wait out front, €6.20 to downtown). Alternatively, just walk (about 10-15 minutes)—beyond the tree-lined plaza, cross the fancy dragon-decorated María Cristina Bridge, turn right onto the busy avenue called Paseo de los Fueros, and follow the Urumea River until the last bridge. The modern, blocky Kursaal Conference Center across the river serves as an easy landmark.

By Bus: A few buses—such as those from the airport—can let you off at pretty Plaza de Gipuzkoa (first stop after crossing the river, in Centro shopping area, one block from the Boulevard, TIs, and old town). But most buses—including those from Bilbao—take you instead to San Sebastian's underground bus station, next to the Renfe train station. To get to the old town from here, go to the María Cristina Bridge and follow the directions from the Renfe station (described above).

By Plane: San Sebastián Airport is beautifully situated along the harbor in the nearby town of Hondarribia, 12 miles east of the city, just across the bay from France (airport code: EAS, www. aena.es). An easy regional bus (#E21) connects the airport to San Sebastián's Plaza de Gipuzkoa, just a block south of the Boulevard and TIs (€2.45, pay driver, 6/day, 35 minutes, http://www. ekialdebus.eus). Other buses connect the airport to San Sebastián's Plaza Gipuzkoa, but #E21 is much faster. A taxi into town costs about €38.

By Car: Take the Amara freeway exit, follow *Centro Ciudad* signs into the city center, and park in a pay lot (many are well

San Sebastián

Accommodations

① Hotel Arrizul Beach & Pensión Kursaal

② Hotel Arrizul Congress

③ Welcome Gros & Launderette

④ Hotel One Shot Tabakalera House

⑤ La Pensión del Mar

⑥ Hotel Niza

Eateries & Other

⑦ Bodega Donostiarra

⑧ To Bar Bergara, Calle Zabaleta Bars & Hogar Dulce Hogar

⑨ To Tedone

⑩ Sakona Coffee Roasters

⑪ Café de la Concha

⑫ Island Boat Tickets

⑬ Catamaran Tickets

⑭ Bike Rental

signed—the Kursaal underground lot is the most central). If you're picking up or returning a rental car, you'll find Europcar at the Renfe train station (+34 943 322 304). Less centrally located are Hertz (Centro Comercial Garbera, Travesía de Garbera 1, take taxi to downtown, +34 943 392 223) and Avis (Hotel Barceló Costa Vasca, Pío Baroja 15, take taxi to downtown, +34 943 461 556).

HELPFUL HINTS

Bookstore: Elkar, an advocate of Basque culture and literature, has two branches on the same street in the old town. Both have a collection of Basque literature, and one has a wide selection of guidebooks, maps, and books in English (Mon-Sat 10:00-14:00 & 16:30-20:00, closed Sun, Calle Fermín Calbetón 21 and 30, +34 943 420 080).

Baggage Storage: It's €5/24 hours of baggage storage at the **bus station** (long hours daily) or at **Navi.net,** an internet café (daily 10:00-21:30, Calle Narrica 12).

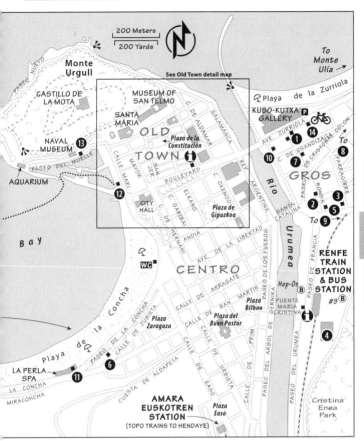

Laundry: In the old town, try **5 à Sec** on the underground level of the smaller building of Bretxa Market (drop-off service, same day if dropped off by 12:00; Mon-Fri 9:30-20:00, Sat until 16:00, closed Sun; +34 943 432 044). Self-service **Garbimatik** is next to Bretxa Market (daily 9:00-22:00, San Lorenzo 6, mobile +34 635 739 795). **Wash & Dry** is in the Gros neighborhood, across the river (self-service daily 8:00-22:00, drop-off Mon-Fri only 9:30-13:00 & 16:00-20:00, Iparragirre 6, +34 943 293 150).

Bike Rental: The city has some great bike lanes and is a good place to enjoy on two wheels. San Sebastián's bike-sharing program, called **dBizi,** offers an occasional-user card that's available at any stand (must load €9 credit for one-day card, €150 hold on credit card, rental fee-€1/hour). Or, try **Sanse Bikes** near the City Hall (€7/2 hours, €10/4 hours, €15/8 hours; Boulevard 25, +34 943 045 229). Another option is **Bici Rent Donosti** (€15/4 hours, afternoon rentals-€6/hour, scooters available in summer; Avenida de Zurriola 22, three blocks across river from TI, mobile +34 639 016 013).

Marijuana: While Spain is famously liberal about marijuana laws, the Basque Country is even more so. Walking around San Sebastián, you'll see "grow shops" sporting the famous green leaf (shopkeepers are helpful if you have questions). The sale of marijuana is still illegal, but marijuana consumption is decriminalized, and people are allowed to grow enough for their personal use at home. With the town's mesmerizing aquarium and delightfully lit bars filled with enticing munchies, it just makes sense.

GETTING AROUND SAN SEBASTIÁN

By Bus: Along the Boulevard at the bottom edge of the old town, you'll find a line of public buses ready to take you anywhere in town; give any driver your destination, and he or she will tell you the number of the bus to catch (€1.80, €2.10 after midnight, pay driver).

Some handy bus routes: #21, #26, and #28 connect the Amara EuskoTren station to the TIs (get off at the Boulevard stop); #5, #16, and #25 begin at the Boulevard/TI stop, go along Playa de la Concha and through residential areas; #16 eventually arrives at the base of the Monte Igueldo funicular. Bus info: www.dbus.eus.

By Taxi: Taxis start at €6.20, which covers most rides in the center. You can't hail a taxi on the street—you must call one (+34 943 404 040 or +34 943 464 646) or find a taxi stand (most convenient along the Boulevard).

Tours in San Sebastián

Walking Tours

The **city-oriented TIs** run English-language walking tours. Options include Essential San Sebastián and Cultural San Sebastián (both €12.50 and 2 hours). Schedules vary—ask and reserve at a TI, call +34 943 481 166, or check www.sansebastianturismo.eus.

Local Guides

Based in San Sebastián, **Agustin Ciriza** leads walking tours of his hometown and guided tours through the Spanish and French Basque Country, with destinations including Bilbao, Hondarribia, Biarritz, and the Biscay Coast. He also offers guided Camino walks, mountain treks, and Rioja region wine tours, as well as *txakolí* tastings (€180/group for city tours, from €15/person for hiking options, mobile +34 686 117 395, https://agustinciriza.com).

Gabriella Ranelli, an American who's lived in San Sebastián for more than 30 years, specializes in culinary tours. She can take you on a sightseeing spin around the old town, along with a walk through the market and best *pintxo* bars (€155/person, 2-person minimum, less for 4 or more people), or on an excursion to nearby towns and wine regions (from €750/day, transportation included for up to 4 people, +34 943 422 163, www.tenedortours.com). Gabriella also organizes cooking classes—where you shop at the market, then join a local chef to cook up some tasty *pintxos* of your own (€265/person, 2-person minimum, less for 4 or more people)—as well as wine tastings (starting at €195/person).

James Scanlan, an American settled in San Sebastián, offers a variety of tours in the city and greater Basque Country. Options range from city walks and *pintxos* tours to themed tours focused on regional history, maritime culture, or in-depth wine experiences (€180/3 hours). He also runs **James in Spain,** offering cycling tours for all levels, both in town and on quiet, charming Basque roads (mobile +34 688 607 545, www.jamesinspain.com).

Itsaso Petrikorena leads food and cultural tours of the city and countryside villages, as well as visits to wineries and cider houses (mobile +34 647 973 231, betitsaso@yahoo.es).

Gastronomic Tours

Mimo San Sebastián offers a half-day gourmet cooking class (prices start at €175/person, including ingredients and wine) and *pintxo* tours that have you hopping from bar to bar (€125, includes food and wine). They also sell a Pintxo Passport to help you explore bars without a guide (€85, Paseo Republica Argentina 4, +34 943 008 070, www.sansebastian.mimofood.com).

Tours on Wheels

Most travelers won't find it necessary in this walkable city, but the **"txu-txu"** tourist train gives you a good overview of San Sebastián (€5, daily 11:00-20:00, mid-Sept-June until 18:30, closed Jan-Feb and Mon off-season, 40-minute round-trip, +34 943 422 973, http://sansebastian.city-tour.com). A faster **hop-on, hop-off bus** with several stops around the city is run by the same company. Buy an all-day €12 ticket on the bus, at the TI, or online (daily 10:30-20:00, shorter hours off-season, handy stop in front of Renfe train station for day-trippers).

Sights in San Sebastián

IN THE OLD TOWN

Huddled in the shadow of its once-protective Monte Urgull, the old town (Parte Vieja, worth ▲▲) is where San Sebastián was born about 1,000 years ago. Because the town burned down in 1813 (as Spain, Portugal, and England fought the French to get Napoleon's brother off the Spanish throne), the architecture you see is generally Neoclassical and uniform. Still, the grid plan of streets hides heavy Baroque and Gothic churches, surprise plazas, and fun little shops, including venerable pastry stores, rugged produce markets, Basque-independence souvenir shops, and seafood-to-go delis. The highlight of the old town is its array of incredibly lively tapas bars—though here these snacks are called *pintxos* (PEEN-chohs; see "Eating in San Sebastián," later). To see the fishing industry in action, wander out to the port (described later).

Throughout the old town, flagpoles mark **"private eating clubs"** (you might occasionally see a club's name displayed, but most are otherwise unmarked). The clubs used to be exclusively male; women are now allowed as invited guests...but never in the kitchen, which remains the men's domain. Basque society is matrilineal and very female-oriented. A husband brings home his paycheck and hands it directly to his wife, who controls the house's purse strings (and everything else). Basque men felt they needed a place where they could congregate and play "king of the castle," so they formed these clubs where members could reserve a table and cook for their friends.

▲Plaza de la Constitución

The old town's main square is where bullfights used to be held. Notice the seat numbering on the balconies: Even if you owned an

apartment here, the city retained rights to the balconies, which it could sell as box seats. (Residents could peek over the paying customers' shoulders.) Above the clock, notice the seal of San Sebastián: a merchant ship with sails billowing in the wind. The city was granted trading rights

by the crown—a reminder of the Basque Country's importance in Spanish seafaring. Inviting café tables crowd the square from all corners.

▲▲Museum of San Telmo (San Telmo Museoa)

This fascinating museum innovatively wrapped a modern facade around a 16th-century Dominican convent and its peaceful cloister. It's now the largest museum of Basque culture in the country and is well worth a visit. Exhibits of archaeological and ethnographic artifacts demonstrate the traditional folkways of Basque life and vividly tell the history of the region. Its art collection features a few old-school gems (El Greco, Rubens, Tintoretto), while 19th- and 20th-century paintings by Basque artists offer an interesting glimpse into the spirit, faces, and natural beauty of these fiercely independent people. Displays lack explanations in English, but portable placards and an English audioguide provide a sufficient overview.

Cost and Hours: €6, free on Tue, includes audioguide, Tue-Sun 10:00-20:00, closed Mon, Plaza Zuloaga 1, +34 943 481 580, www.santelmomuseoa.eus.

Visiting the Museum: The museum's layout takes you through the temporary exhibitions first—often focusing on Basque art movements. Or you can enter directly into Section 1, within the church of the original convent. It houses 11 exceptional varnish-on-metal paintings by Spanish artist José María Sert; the light reflecting off this artwork bathes the church in a hauntingly warm glow. Commissioned in 1929, when the convent was originally converted into a museum, these "Sert Canvases" are passionate depictions of epic Basque moments and traditions.

Breeze through Section 2, which features steles or funerary markers, and tuck into Section 3, where traditional Basque tools and time-honored apparel are smartly displayed. A fine ship model is part of a high-tech exhibit illustrating the far reaches of seafaring Basque explorers.

Continue upstairs to Section 4 to cover the basics of Basque social history and gain a bird's-eye view of the Sert Canvases. You'll also learn how the Basque people transitioned from a rural lifestyle to urban modernity in the 19th and 20th centuries. Enjoy a look at Basque-manufactured products—the Kenmores and Frigidaires of Spain—along with a little pop culture.

Paintings from the 15th to 19th centuries are displayed in Section 5 on the top-most floor, giving you a chronological look at respectable works from several well-known (and many lesser-known) Spanish artists.

▲Bretxa Public Market (Mercado de la Bretxa)

Wandering through the public market is a fun way to get in touch with San Sebastián and Basque culture. Although the sandstone market building facing the Boulevard and the large, former Pescadería building have both been converted into a modern shopping complex, the farmers' produce market thrives here (lined up outside along the side of the mall), as does the fish and meat market (underground).

Hours: Mon-Sat 8:00-21:00, closed Sun, Bretxa Plaza.

Visiting the Market: To get to the modern fish-and-meat market, walk past the produce vendors (look under the eaves of the building to see what the farmers are selling), and find a big glass cube in the square, where an escalator takes you down into the market.

At the bottom of the escalator, take a left and stroll to the back of the market to explore the **fresh-fish stands**—often with

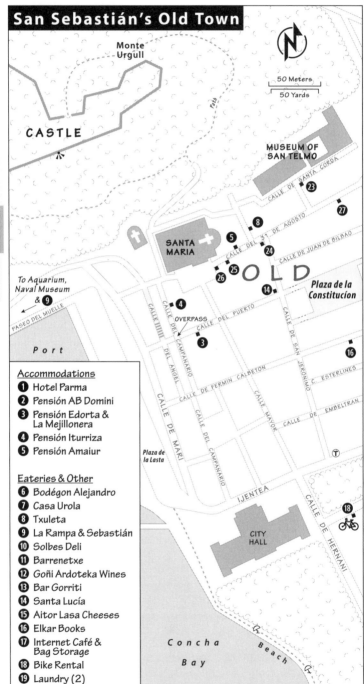

San Sebastián's Old Town

SPANISH BASQUE COUNTRY

Monte Urgull

CASTLE

MUSEUM OF SAN TELMO

SANTA MARIA

To Aquarium, Naval Museum & 9

Port

OLD

Plaza de la Constitución

OVERPASS

Plaza de la Lasta

CITY HALL

Concha Bay

Beach

Accommodations
1. Hotel Parma
2. Pensión AB Domini
3. Pensión Edorta & La Mejillonera
4. Pensión Iturriza
5. Pensión Amaiur

Eateries & Other
6. Bodégon Alejandro
7. Casa Urola
8. Txuleta
9. La Rampa & Sebastián
10. Solbes Deli
11. Barrenetxe
12. Goñi Ardoteka Wines
13. Bar Gorriti
14. Santa Lucía
15. Aitor Lasa Cheeses
16. Elkar Books
17. Internet Café & Bag Storage
18. Bike Rental
19. Laundry (2)

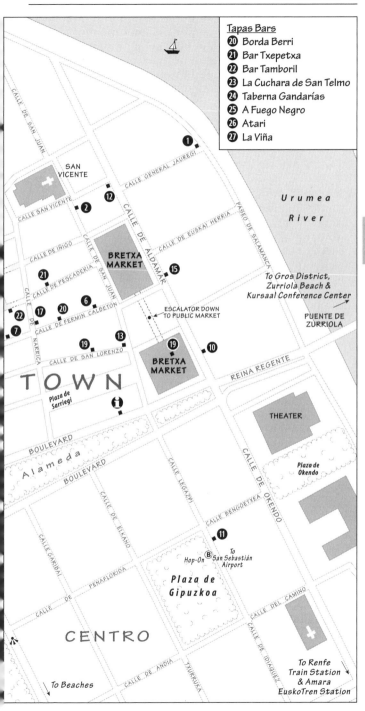

Tapas Bars
20 Borda Berri
21 Bar Txepetxa
22 Bar Tamboril
23 La Cuchara de San Telmo
24 Taberna Gandarías
25 A Fuego Negro
26 Atari
27 La Viña

the catch of the day set up in cute little scenes. Few fish stands are open on Monday because boats don't go out on Sunday; even fishermen need a day off. Take a left, go to the end of the stalls, and look for the fish stand called Bacalaos Uranzu. In the display, you'll see different cuts of *bacalao* (cod). Entire books have been written about the importance of cod to the evolution of seafaring in Europe. The fish could be preserved in salt to feed sailors on ever-longer trips into the North Atlantic, allowing them to venture beyond the continental shelf (into deeper waters where they couldn't catch fresh fish). Cod was also popular among Catholic landlubbers on Fridays. Today cod remains a Basque staple. People still buy the salted version, which must be soaked for 48 hours (and the water changed three times) to become edible. If you're in a rush, you can buy desalted cod...but at a cost in flavor. There's a free **WC** in the market—just ask "*¿Dónde está el servicio, por favor?*"

When you're done exploring, take the escalator up, turn left, and cross the street to the **Aitor Lasa** cheese shop at Aldamar 12 (closed Sun, +34 943 430 354). Pass the fragrant piles of mushrooms at the entrance and head back to the display case, showing off the Basque specialty of *idiazábal*—raw sheep's milk cheese. Notice the wide variety, which depends on the specific region it came from, whether it's smoked or cured, and for how long it's been cured *(curación)*. If you're planning a picnic, this is a very local (and expensive) ingredient. To try the cheese that won first prize a few years back in the Ordizia International Cheese Competition, ask for "*El queso con el premio de Ordizia, por favor.*" The owners are evangelical about the magic of combining the local cheese with walnuts and *dulce de manzana* homemade apple jam.

AT THE PORT

At the west end of the old town, protected by Monte Urgull, is the port. Take the passage through the wall at the appropriately named Calle Puerto, and jog right along the level, portside promenade, Paseo del Muelle. You'll pass fishing boats unloading the catch of the day (with hungry locals looking on), salty sailors' pubs, and fishermen mending nets. Also along this strip are the skippable Naval Museum

and the entertaining aquarium. Trails to the top of Monte Urgull are just above this scene, near Santa María Church (or climb the stairs next to the aquarium).

Cruises

Small boats cruise from the old town's port to the island in the bay (Isla de Santa Clara), where you can hike the trails and have lunch at the lone café, or pack a picnic before setting sail. **Motoras de la Isla** offers two options: the direct red *(roja)* route to the island (€4 round-trip, small ferry departs June-Sept only, every half-hour 10:00-20:00) and the blue *(azul)* route, which cruises the bay for 30 minutes in a glass-bottom boat before dropping passengers off (€6.50 round-trip, hourly 12:00-19:30, +34 943 000 450, www.motorasdelaisla.com). The *Ciudad San Sebastián* catamaran gives 40-minute tours of the bay from Monte Urgull to Zurriola Beach (€12, hourly in summer 12:00-20:00, fewer in spring and fall, none in winter; +34 943 287 932, www.ciudadsansebastian.com).

Naval Museum (Museo Naval)

This small museum is mostly interesting for its 18th-century building—one of the few that survived the 1813 siege of the city and where port activities were monitored. Its two floors house temporary exhibits related to the city's connection to the sea.

Cost and Hours: €3, free on Thu, borrow English description at entry, Tue-Sat 10:00-14:00 & 16:00-19:00, Sun 11:00-14:00, closed Mon, Paseo del Muelle 24, +34 943 430 051, www.itsasmuseoa.eus.

▲▲Aquarium

San Sebastián's aquarium is surprisingly good. Upstairs are displays on whaling, shipbuilding, legal versus illegal pirating, fishing, and local oceanography (with thorough English descriptions). Downstairs, a mesmerizing 45-foot-long tunnel is filled with more than 30 local species of sea life, flopping and flying over you in a tank holding nearly 400,000 gallons of water. Several smaller tanks are homes to octopus, slowly tumbling jellyfish, and tropical species—local kids see them and holler, "Nemo!"

Cost and Hours: €13, €6.50 for kids ages 4-12; daily 10:00-21:00, closes earlier in off-season, last entry one hour before closing; stuffy-yet-helpful audioguide-€2, at the end of Paseo del Muelle, +34 943 440 099, www.aquariumss.com.

▲Monte Urgull

Green and leafy, this city park watches over the old town. The once-mighty castle (Castillo de la Mota) atop the hill deterred most attackers, allowing the city to prosper in the Middle Ages.

The **Casa de la Historia** museum within the castle covers San Sebastián history; it has mildly interesting displays on the ground floor and access to the statue of Christ's view over the city. There are also 13 delightful videos available in English—created for the 200th anniversary of the city's devastating fire of 1813, each eight-minute film features San Sebastián youth sharing their city's important historical moments (free to enter museum, English pamphlet, Wed-Sun 10:00-17:30, closed in winter and Mon-Tue year-round, +34 943 428 417).

Maps scattered throughout the **park** provide good and basic information about the fortress. Seek out the crumbling memorial to British soldiers who gave their lives to defend the city from Napoleon. The best views from the hill are not from the statue of Christ, but from the **Battery of Santiago** ramparts (to Christ's far right), just above the port's aquarium. Picnickers can enjoy their lunch along the walls and on benches peppering the grassy battery park, or walk to the westernmost point of the battery to the free-spirited **Café El Polvorín** for simple salads, sandwiches, good sangria, and picturesque vistas.

A walkway allows you to stroll the mountain's entire perimeter near sea level. This route is continuous from Hotel Parma to the aquarium and offers an enjoyable after-dinner wander. You can also walk a bit higher up over the port (along the white railing)—called the *paseo de los curas*, or "priest's path," where the clergy could stroll unburdened by the rabble in the streets below (access from just behind the aquarium). These paths are technically open only from sunrise to sunset (daily 8:00-21:00, Oct-April until 19:30), but you can often access them even later.

THE BEACH AND BEYOND
▲▲La Concha Beach and Promenade

The shell-shaped Playa de la Concha, the pride of San Sebastián, has one of Europe's loveliest stretches of sand. Lined with a two-mile-long promenade, it allows even backpackers to feel aristocratic. Although it's pretty empty off-season, sunbathers pack its shores in summer. But year-round it's surprisingly devoid of eateries and money-grubbing businesses. There are free showers, and *cabinas* provide lockers, showers, and shade

for a fee. For a century, the lovingly painted wrought-iron balustrade that stretches the length of the promenade has been a symbol of the city; it shows up on everything from jewelry to headboards. It's shaded by tamarisk trees, with branches carefully pruned into knotty bulbs each winter that burst into leafy shade-giving canopies in the summer—another symbol of the city. **$$ Café de la Concha** serves reasonably priced, mediocre food, but you can't beat the location of its terrace overlooking the beach (€15 weekday lunch special, +34 943 473 600).

The **Miramar Palace and Park** divides the crescent beach in the middle at Pico de Loro (Parrot's Beak). This is where Queen María Cristina held court when she summered here in the early 1900s. Today the palace is home to summer classes for the Basque Studies University, as well as a music school. The gardens are open to the public.

La Perla Spa

The spa overlooking the beach attracts a less royal crowd today and appeals mostly to visitors interested in sampling "the curative properties of the sea." You can enjoy its Talasso Fitness Circuit, featuring a hydrotherapy pool, a relaxation pool, a panoramic hot tub, cold-water pools, a seawater steam sauna, a dry sauna, and a relaxation area.

Cost and Hours: 2-hour fitness circuit-€28, Mon-Sat 9:00-21:00, Sun until 15:00, €3 caps and €1.20 rental towels, bring a swimsuit or buy one there, on the beach at the center of the crescent, Paseo de la Concha, +34 943 458 856, www.la-perla.net.

Monte Igueldo

For commanding city views (if you ignore the tacky amusements on top), ride the funicular or hike up Monte Igueldo, a mirror image of Monte Urgull. The views over San Sebastián, along the coast, and into the distant green mountains are sensational day or night. The entrance to the funicular is on the road behind  the tennis club on the far western end of Playa de Ondarreta, which extends from Playa de la Concha to the west.

Cost and Hours: Funicular-€3.75 round-trip; changeable hours but roughly April-Sept daily 10:00-21:00; Oct-March Mon-Fri 11:00-18:00, Sat-Sun until 20:00. If you drive to the top, you'll pay €2.35 to enter.

Getting There: Bus #16 takes you from Plaza de Gipuzkoa in the old town to the base of the funicular in about 10 minutes. If you'd rather do the half-hour hike to the top, start at the Tenis bus stop before the funicular and follow the yellow arrows uphill along a road and then on a smaller path. It can be muddy after a rainy day, but it's well worth the walk through the lush forest. Near the top, take a right at the asphalt road to reach the viewpoint.

SPANISH BASQUE COUNTRY

Peine del Viento

Besides the gorgeous view from the top of Monte Igueldo, another classic San Sebastián scene is at this group of three statues by native son Eduardo Chillida (1924-2002). From the base of the Monte Igueldo funicular, walk around the tennis court complex to the edge of the beach. Curly steel prongs "comb the wind" (as the sculptures' name means) among crashing waves. Chillida lived and died on Monte Igueldo, so these sculptures are now considered a memorial to one of Spain's most internationally recognized modern sculptors.

IN GROS

Gros and Zurriola Beach

The district of Gros, just east across the river from the old town, offers a distinctly Californian vibe. Literally a dump not long ago (gross indeed), today it has a surfing scene on Zurriola Beach (popular with students and German tourists) and a futuristic conference center (described next).

▲Kursaal Conference Center and Kubo-Kutxa Gallery

These two Lego-like boxes mark the spot of what was once a grand casino, torn down by Franco to discourage gambling. Many locals wanted to rebuild it as it once was, in a similar style to the turn-of-the-20th-century buildings in the Centro, but—in an effort to keep up with the postmodern trends in Bilbao—city leaders opted instead for Rafael Moneo's striking contemporary design. The complex is supposed to resemble the angular rocks that make up the town's breakwater. The Kursaal houses a theater, conference facilities, some gift shops and travel agencies, and a restaurant; it also hosts many events for the San Sebastián Film Festival. The Kubo-Kutxa Gallery, located in a small cube farthest from the river, offers temporary exhibits by international artists and promotes contemporary Basque artists. Each exhibit is complemented by a 10-minute video that plays continuously in the gallery theater (free, Tue-Sun 11:30-13:00 & 17:00-21:00, closed Mon, no-midday break on summer weekends, +34 943 251 939, www.sala-kubo-aretoa.eus.

Tabakalera International Culture Center

An old tobacco factory next to the Renfe train station has been converted into an international center for contemporary culture oozing with a young, artistic vibe. The center hosts the Basque Language Institute, various contemporary art exhibitions from both local and international artists, and screenings during the San Sebastián Film Festival. There are shops and a café on the bottom floor, and the roof terrace on the top floor has knockout views of the river and city skyline. To get there, take bus #9 from the Boulevard stop in the old town and get off at the Frantziskotarrak stop (free, Mon-

Fri 9:00-21:00, Sat 10:00-22:00, Sun 10:00-21:00, Andre Zigar-rogileak Plaza 1, +34 943 118 855, www.tabakalera.eu).

Sleeping in San Sebastián

Rates in San Sebastián are some of the highest in Spain. They can skyrocket in summer and during the town's film festival in September. During peak season, hotels often require a minimum stay of two to three nights. Since breakfast is often not included, I've recommended some good options elsewhere in town (see "Eating in San Sebastián," later).

IN OR NEAR THE OLD TOWN

For locations, see the "San Sebastián's Old Town" map, earlier.

$$$$ Hotel Parma is a business-class place with 26 fine rooms and family-run attention to detail and service. It stands stately on the edge of the old town, away from the bar-scene noise, and overlooks the river and a surfing beach (RS%, air-con, modern lounge, pay parking nearby, Paseo de Salamanca 10, +34 943 428 893, www.hotelparma.com, hotelparma@hotelparma.com; Iñaki, Pino, Maria Eugenia, and Eider).

$$$ Pensión AB Domini neighbors Bretxa Market and San Telmo Museum. It delightfully mixes traditional, bare-stone walls with contemporary decor. Three of its six rooms have views toward the museum—unique in the narrow-laned old town. With only two *pintxo* bars nearby, it's one of the quieter hotels in town, but bring earplugs for Saturdays (some rooms with shared bath, discounted parking, San Juan 8, second floor, +34 943 420 431, www.abpensiones.es, reservas@abpensiones.es).

$$ Pensión Edorta ("Edward"), family owned and run with care deep in the old town, elegantly mixes wood, brick, and color in nine stylish rooms (elevator, Calle del Puerto 15, +34 943 423 773, www.pensionedorta.com, info@pensionedorta.com, Javier).

$$ Pensión Iturriza is no Old World *pensión*—its six small, minimalist rooms have modern fixtures and were designed with feng shui in mind. This is a restful and quiet place (Calle Campanario 10, +34 943 562 959, www.pensioniturriza.com, info@pensioniturriza.com).

$ Pensión Amaiur, in the oldest building in the old town, has tilting wooden stairs that lead to a flowery interior with long, narrow halls and 12 great-value rooms. Some rooms face a *frontón* (*pelota* court), while a couple have private balconies facing the street. There are common rooms on both floors to prepare meals—a great spot to hang out and share travel tips. Bring earplugs to block out noise from the tapas-going crowd, or ask for an interior room (cheaper rooms with shared bath, next to Santa María Church at

Calle 31 de Agosto 44, +34 943 429 654, www.pensionamaiur. com, info@pensionamaiur.com).

ACROSS THE RIVER, IN GROS

The pleasant Gros district—San Sebastián's "uptown"—is marked by the super-modern, blocky Kursaal conference center. The nearby Zurriola Beach is popular with surfers and has a thriving *pintxos* scene and good restaurants. Most of these hotels are less than a five-minute walk from the old town. For locations, see the "San Sebastián" map, earlier.

$$$$ Hotel Arrizul Beach is bright and fresh, with fashionable, minimalist decor in each of its 12 rooms (air-con, elevator, pricey nearby underground parking, Peña y Goñi 1, +34 943 322 804, www.arrizul.com, info@hotelarrizulbeach.com). Just up the street, closer to the train and bus stations, **$$$$ Hotel Arrizul Congress** is run by the same friendly staff and has a similar style (family rooms, air-con, elevator, Ronda 3, +34 943 327 026, www. hotelarrizulcongress.com, info@hotelarrizulcongress.com).

$$$$ Welcome Gros is five blocks from the beach and has 15 rooms with minimal but stylish decor, plus 11 apartments with daily cleaning. Stay in for their high-quality breakfast (air-con, elevator, Iparraguirre 3, +34 943 326 954, www.welcomegros.com; for apartments see www.groscity.com, info@welcomegros.com).

$$$ Hotel One Shot Tabakalera House is an artsy hotel in the same building as the International Culture Center, the city's old tobacco factory. It is conveniently located next to the Renfe train station and is a 20-minute walk from the old town. The rooms are hip and contemporary with a colorful design (air-con, discounted parking, fitness room, Mandasko Dukearen 52, +34 943 930 028, www.hoteloneshottabakalerahouse.com, tabakalerahouse@ oneshothotels.com).

$$ Pensión Kursaal has 21 basic, contemporary, and crisp rooms in a historic building just across from the beach (elevator, pay parking, Peña y Goñi 2, +34 943 292 666, www.pensionkursaal. com, info@pensionkursaal.com).

$$ La Pensión del Mar has six bright rooms on a quiet street just a 10-minute walk from the old town. There is small common kitchen and free coffee and tea (elevator, discounted parking, two rooms with shared bathroom, Tomas Gros 3, +34 943 359 970, www.lapensiondelmar.es, info@lapensiondelmar.es).

ON THE BEACH

$$$$ Hotel Niza, set in the middle of Playa de la Concha, is often booked well in advance. Half of its 40 rooms (some with balconies) overlook the bay. From its chandeliered and plush lounge, a classic 1911 elevator takes you to comfortable pastel rooms with wedding-cake molding (only streetside rooms have air-con, fans on request, pay parking—must reserve in advance, Zubieta 56, +34 943 426 663, www.hotelniza.com, reservas@hotelniza.com). The breakfast room has a sea view and doubles as a bar with light snacks throughout the day (Bar Narru, long hours daily).

Eating in San Sebastián

Basque food is regarded as some of the best in Spain, and San Sebastián is the culinary capital of the Basque Country. (For tips on Basque cuisine, see the "Basque Country Cuisine Scene" section at the beginning of this chapter.) San Sebastián is proud of its many Michelin-rated fine-dining establishments, but they require a big commitment of time and money. Most casual visitors will prefer to hop from pub to pub through the old town, following the crowds between Basque-font signs. I've listed a couple of solid traditional restaurants, but for the best value and memories, I'd order top-end dishes with top-end wine in top-end bars. Some places close for siesta in the late afternoon and early evening.

IN THE OLD TOWN

For locations of Old Town eateries, see the "San Sebastián's Old Town" map, earlier.

Pintxo Bar-Hopping

San Sebastián's old town provides the ideal backdrop for tapas-hopping; just wander the streets and sidle up to the bar in the liveliest spot. Calle Fermín Calbetón has the best concentration of bars;

the streets San Jerónimo and 31 de Agosto are also good. I've listed these top-notch places in order as you progress deeper into the old town. Note that there are plenty of other options along the way. Before you begin, study the *txikiteo* sidebar, later. Unless otherwise noted, these places are open from around noon to 15:00, close for the afternoon, then reopen in the evening.

$$ Borda Berri (loosely, "New Mountain Hut") features a

more low-key ambience and top-quality *pintxos*. There are only a few items at the bar; check out the chalkboard menu for today's options, order, and the two chefs/owners will cook it fresh. The specialty here is melt-in-your-mouth beef cheeks *(carrillera de ternera)* in a red-wine sauce, risotto with wild mushrooms, and foie gras (grilled goose liver) with apple jelly, which is even better paired with a glass of their best red wine (closed Mon, Calle Fermín Calbetón 12, +34 943 430 342).

$$ Bar Txepetxa is *the* place for anchovies. A plastic circle displaying a variety of *antxoas* tapas makes choosing your anchovy treat easy. These fish are fresh—not cured and salted like those most Americans hate (Sun lunch only, Tue dinner only, closed Mon, Calle Pescadería 5, +34 943 422 227).

$$ Bar Tamboril is a traditional spot right on the main square, favored for its seafood, mushrooms *(txampis tamboril),* and anchovy tempura along with its good prices. Their list of hot *pintxos* (grab the little English menu on the bar) makes you want to break the one-tapa-per-stop rule (Calle Pescadería 2, +34 943 423 507).

$$$ La Cuchara de San Telmo, whose cooks are taught by big-name Basque chef Alex Mondiel, is a cramped place that devotes as much space to its thriving kitchen as its bar. It has nothing precooked and set on the bar—order your mini gourmet plates with a spirit of adventure from the constantly changing blackboard. Their foie gras with apple jelly is rightfully famous (lunch only on weekends, closed Mon, tucked away on a lonely alley called Santa Corda behind Museum of San Telmo at Calle 31 de Agosto 28, +34 943 420 840).

$$ Taberna Gandarías is a great place for savory traditional *pintxos* in a lively but easygoing atmosphere. The personable blue-shirted fellas tending to you will patiently explain the food options. Consider a *media ración* (half-order) of the perfectly done *ibérico* ham. They serve food more hours than most (some gluten-free options, daily 11:00-24:00, Calle 31 de Agosto 23, +34 943 426 362).

$$$ A Fuego Negro is cool and upscale compared to the others, with an edgier vibe. Check the wall behind the bar for what's available (or ask for a menu) and scan the blackboard-like columns for their good wine list and drinks. They have a knack for mixing gourmet pretentiousness with whimsy here: Try their *arroz, tomate, y un huevo* (risotto with tomato and egg); *bakailu* (cod); and *regaliz* (licorice ice cream) trio for a unique taste-bud experience (closed Mon, Calle 31 de Agosto 31, mobile +34 650 135 373). An inviting little section in the back makes this a sit-down dining opportunity.

$$ Atari offers a handful of comfortable tables and large windows. In warm weather, sit at outdoor tables across from Santa María Church. They have *pintxos* and *raciones: Pulpo con piment Espelette* (octopus with Espelette peppers) and *foie a la plancha* (grilled duck liver) are just a couple of the delights on the menu (daily 12:00-23:30, Calle Mayor 18, can also enter on corner of Calle 31 de Agosto, +34 943 440 792).

$$ La Mejillonera is famous among students for its big, cheap beers, *patatas bravas,* and mussels (*"tigres"* are the spicy favorite). A long, skinny stainless-steel bar and lots of photos make ordering easy—this is my only recommended bar where you pay when served. Throw your mussel shells on the floor like the boisterous locals (Calle del Puerto 15, +34 943 428 465).

$$ La Viña is a reliable option for a mix of traditional and modern *pintxos.* Rub elbows with locals and top off your meal with an airy and decadent slice of cheesecake that's big enough to share (daily, closed Nov and last week of June, Calle 31 de Agosto 3, +34 943 427 495).

Restaurants in the Old Town

$$$ Bodégon Alejandro is a good spot for modern Basque cuisine in a sleek-yet-cozy cellar setting (Tue-Sat 13:00-15:30 & 20:30-22:30, closed Sun-Mon, in old town on Calle Fermín Calbetón 4, +34 943 427 158).

$$$ Casa Urola is a must for San Sebastián gastronomy enthusiasts. Chef Pablo's updated versions of traditional Basque dishes even persuade other local chefs to eat here after finishing their shifts. Much of the exquisite menu changes seasonally. The peaceful upstairs dining room has a contemporary elegance (reservations recommended). Without reservations, go downstairs—there are few tables, so most diners eat standing at the bar (*media ración*—half-portion—available for several dishes, extensive wine list; Wed-Mon 13:00-16:00 & 20:00-23:00, bar open until late, closed Tue; Fermín Calbetón 20, +34 943 441 371, www.casaurolajatetxea.es).

$$ Txuleta is tucked away on a small plaza near Santa Maria Church. While the service can be hit or miss, this restaurant excels at grilled meats and seasonal *pintxos* that are worth the hefty price. Be adventurous and try the *kokotxas* (hake cheeks). The glass-enclosed terrace provides lots of seating (closed Mon evening and Tue, Plaza de la Trinidad 2, +34 943 441 007, www.txuletarestaurante.com).

Seafood Along the Port: For seafood with a salty sailor's view, check out the half-dozen hardworking, local-feeling restaurants that line the harbor on the way to the aquarium. **$$$$ La Rampa** is an upscale eatery, specializing in crab *(txangurro)* and lobster dishes and seafood *parillada* (closed Wed, Paseo del Muelle 26, +34 943 421 652, www.restaurantelarampa.com). Also along here, locals like **$$$ Sebastián** (more traditional, closed Tue).

Do the *Txikiteo:* A Tapas Cheat Sheet

Txikiteo (chih-kee-TAY-oh) is the Basque word for hopping from bar to bar, enjoying small sandwiches and tiny snacks (*pintxos*, PEEN-chohs) and glasses of wine. Local competition drives small bars to lay out the most appealing array of *pintxos.* The selection is amazing, but the key to eating well here is going for the *pintxos calientes*—the hot tapas advertised on blackboards and cooked to order. Tapas are best, freshest, and accompanied by the most vibrant crowd from 12:00 to 14:00 and from 20:00 to 22:30. Watch what's being served—the locals know each bar's specialty. No matter how much you like a place, just order one dish; you want to be mobile.

Later in the evening, bars get more crowded and challenging for tourists. To get service amid the din, speak loudly and directly (little sweet voices get ignored), with no extra words. Expect to share everything. Double-dipping is encouraged. It's rude to put a dirty napkin on the table; it belongs in the small bins or directly on the floor.

Basque tapas bars distinguish themselves by laying out big platters of help-yourself goodies. This user-friendly system lets you point to—or simply take—what looks good, rather than navigating a menu. If you can't get the bartender's attention to serve you a particular *pintxo,* don't be shy—watch other people; if they are serving themselves, grab what you want and a napkin, and munch away. You pay when you leave; just keep a mental note of

RESTAURANTS AND PINTXO BARS IN GROS

For locations, see the "San Sebastián" map, earlier.

$$ Bodega Donostiarra has been a San Sebastián institution since 1928. Locals flock here for sit-down meals with freshly made Spanish tortillas, meats of the grilled and cured varieties, and seafood. For a quick bite, head to their original zinc bar for *pintxos* or a *sandwich completo* with tuna, onions, and anchovies (Mon-Thu 9:30-23:00, Fri-Sat until 24:00, closed Sun, Calle Peña y Goñi 13, +34 943 011 380).

$$ Bar Bergara serves refined *pintxos* in a casually cool setting. Originally run by *chef-savante* Patxi Bergara, his nephews Monty and Esteban now continue the ethic of serving award-winning *pintxos* that are "eye-catching, original, and petite enough to eat in two bites." Cold snacks are artfully displayed on the bar, while *pintxos calientes* are made when ordered. Ask for an English menu (daily 9:30-16:00 & 18:00-24:00, to-go sandwiches available, General Artetxe 8, +34 943 275 026).

Tedone is one of the few quality vegetarian options in this city

the tapas you've eaten. There's a code of honor. Everyone is part of the extended Basque family. In fact, places that have you fill your plate and pay before eating are generally to be avoided.

If you want a meal instead of *pintxos,* some bars—even ones that look only like bars from the street—have attached dining rooms, usually in the back.

Here are a few terms unique to Basque bars:

pintxos: tapas (small plates)

antxoas: anchovies (not the cured, heavily salted kind you always hated)

txampis (CHAHM-pees): mushrooms

txangurro (chan-GOO-roh): spider crab (or imitation crab), often mixed with onions, tomatoes, and wine, served hot or made into a spread to put on bread

marmitako: tuna stew

ttoro: seafood stew

cazuelas: hot meal-size servings (like *raciones* in Spanish)

txakolí (chah-koh-LEE): fresh white wine, poured from high to aerate it and to add sparkle. Good with seafood, and therefore fits the local cuisine well.

zurito (thoo-REE-toh): small beer

Zenbat da?: "How much?" (to ask for the bill)

SPANISH BASQUE COUNTRY

of *gastronomía.* Hiding out on a tiny lane, this health-conscious eatery dishes up flavorful organic options that are truly Basque (closed Sun, Corta 10, +34 943 273 561).

Thursday Night Party Scene: Every Thursday in Gros, university students and those who want to save some euros brave the masses for *pintxo-pote* (PEEN-cho POH-teh). Because of the increased popularity of gastronomy in San Sebastián, locals, who often eat out regularly, want a good deal for food and drinks. Bars, particularly along **Calle Zabaleta** (between Gran Vía and Avenida Navarra) and parallel streets, offer a drink (usually beer or wine) and a basic *pintxo* for €2. It's basically a happy-hour scene that spills out onto the streets. Just follow the crowds and remember that this isn't just sustenance, it's a social event (19:00-23:00).

PICNICS AND TAKEOUT

A picnic on the beach or atop Monte Urgull is a tempting option. You can assemble a bang-up spread at the **Bretxa Public Market** at Plaza de Sarriegi (described earlier).

Solbes, just across the street from the Bretxa Public Market, has a reputation as *the* gourmet deli store in the old town. There's a remarkable wine selection in the back cellar, plus high-quality cured meats and cheeses out front. Be sure to price fruits and veggies on the scale yourself to avoid confusion at checkout (Mon-Sat 9:00-20:30, Sun until 14:30, Calle Aldamar 4, +34 943 427 818).

Classic **Barrenetxe** has an amazing array of breads, prepared foods, and some of the best desserts in town. You can also grab a coffee in the bar section. In business since 1699, their somewhat formal service is justified. Try their specialty—*Txintxorro,* which is almond cake with orange flavoring—you won't regret it (daily 8:00-20:30, Plaza de Gipuzcoa 9, +34 943 424 482).

For wine, head to **Goñi Ardoteka,** with its ample selection of quality Spanish wines. The three owners (and brothers) Asier, Nerea, and Hamaya are true wine lovers and are happy to give their recommendations (Mon-Fri 10:00-14:00 & 16:30-19:30, Sat 10:30-14:00, closed Sun, Calle Aldamar 3, +34 943 211 597).

BREAKFAST

If your hotel doesn't provide breakfast—or even if it does—consider one of these old-town places. The first is a traditional stand-up bar; the second is a greasy spoon. If you're staying in Gros, consider Hogar Dulce Hogar or Sakona Coffee Roasters.

$$ Bar Gorriti, delightfully local, is packed with market workers and shoppers starting their day. You'll stand at the bar and choose a hot-off-the-grill *francesca jamón* omelet (fluffy, tiny omelet sandwich topped with a slice of ham) and other goodies. This and a good cup of coffee make for a very Basque breakfast. By the time you get there for breakfast, many market workers will be taking their midmorning break (breakfast served Mon-Sat 7:00-10:00, closed Sun, facing the side of the big white market building at San Juan 3, +34 943 428 353).

$$ Santa Lucía, a 1950s-style diner, is ideal for a cheap old town breakfast or *churros* break (*churros* are like deep-fried doughnut sticks that can be dipped in pudding-like hot chocolate). Photos of two dozen different breakfasts decorate the walls, and plates of fresh *churros* keep patrons happy (daily 8:30-21:30, Calle del Puerto 6, +34 943 425 019).

In Gros: $$ Hogar Dulce Hogar (Home Sweet Home) is a solid breakfast option that serves other delightful sweet and savory treats throughout the day. If *torrija* (a decadently dense version of French toast) is on the menu, go for it. There's ample seating in this eatery where rustic meets hipster (daily 8:30-21:30, Calle Bermingham 1 at Calle Zabaleta, +34 943 246 681).

By the river close to the Kursaal is **$ Sakona Coffee Roasters,** specializing in good coffee with a modest selection of sandwiches and a tasty *tarta de queso*. Their coffee is made with beans from their own roastery in Irún (daily 9:00-18:00, Ramón María Lili 2, +34 943 046 457).

San Sebastián Connections

BY TRAIN

San Sebastián has two train stations: Renfe and Amara EuskoTren (described under "Arrival in San Sebastián" on page 13). The station you use depends on your destination.

Renfe Station: This station handles long-distance destinations within Spain (most of which require reservations). Connections include **Irún** (3/day, 30 minutes), **Madrid** (6/day, 5-8 hours), **Burgos** (6/day, 3 hours), **León** (1/day direct, 5 hours, more with transfer), **Pamplona** (2/day direct, 2 hours, more with transfer), **Salamanca** (6/day, some direct, 7 hours), **Barcelona** (2/day, 6 hours), **Santiago de Compostela** (2/day direct, 10.5 hours).

Amara EuskoTren Station: If you're going into France, take the regional Topo train (which leaves from Amara EuskoTren station) over the French border into **Hendaye** (usually 2/hour, 35 minutes). From Hendaye, you can connect to France's SNCF network (www.sncf.com), where connections include **Paris** (5/day direct, 5 hours, more with transfer in Dax or Bordeaux). Unfortunately, the Amara EuskoTren station doesn't have information on Paris-bound trains from Hendaye. EuskoTren tickets to Hendaye must be used within two hours of purchase.

Also leaving from San Sebastián's Amara EuskoTren station are slow regional trains to destinations in Spain's Basque region, including **Bilbao** (hourly, 2.5 hours—the bus is faster). Although the train ride from San Sebastián to Bilbao takes twice as long as the bus, it passes through more interesting countryside. The Basque Country shows off its trademark green and gray: lush green vegetation and gray clouds. It's an odd mix of heavy industrial factories, small homegrown veggie gardens, streams, and every kind of livestock you can imagine. EuskoTren info: +34 902 543 210, www.euskotren.eus.

BY BUS

The underground bus station is conveniently located next to the Renfe train station (across the river, just east of the Centro district).

Different companies offer services to different destinations, with some overlap. Pesa serves the majority of the region from Bayonne to Bilbao (www.pesa.net). Alsa serves a few Basque Country destinations, Madrid, Burgos, and León (www.alsa.es). Mon-Bus serves Barcelona (www.monbus.es).

From San Sebastián, buses go to **Bilbao** (2/hour, hourly on

SPANISH BASQUE COUNTRY

weekends, 1.5 hours, Pesa; morning buses fill with tourists, commuters, and students—buy your ticket the day before; once in Bilbao, buses leave you at the Intermodal station with easy tram connections to the Guggenheim modern-art museum); **Bilbao Airport** (hourly, 1.5 hours, Pesa), **Pamplona** (8-10/day, 1 hour, Alsa or Mon-Bus), **León** (1/day, 6 hours, Alsa), **Madrid** (8/day, 6 hours direct, otherwise 7 hours; a few departures direct to Madrid's Barajas Airport, 5.5 hours; Alsa), **Burgos** (7/day, 3.5 hours, Alsa), **Barcelona** (2/day and 1 at night, 7 hours, Mon-Bus).

Buses to French Basque Country: French company BlaBlaBus runs buses to **St-Jean-de-Luz,** which then continue on to **Biarritz** and **Bayonne** (4/day, fewer on Sun, depart from outside the Renfe train station—not underground, www.blablabus.com), as do Spanish companies Pesa (2/day) and Alsa (5/day). General travel times from San Sebastián are 45 minutes to St-Jean-de-Luz, 1.25 hours to Biarritz, and 1.5 hours to Bayonne.

Bay of Biscay

Between the Spanish Basque cities of San Sebastián and Bilbao is a beautiful countryside of rolling green hills and a scenic, jagged coastline that looks almost Celtic. Aside from a scenic joyride, this area merits a visit for the cute fishing and resort town of Lekeitio.

FROM SAN SEBASTIÁN TO BILBAO

San Sebastián and Bilbao are connected in about an hour and a quarter by the AP-8 toll road. While speedy and scenic, this route is nothing compared with some of the free, but slower, back roads with lots of twists and turns that connect the two towns.

If side-tripping from San Sebastián to Bilbao, you can drive directly there on AP-8 in the morning. But going home to San Sebastián, consider this more scenic route: Take AP-8 until the turnoff for Guernica (look for *Amorebieta/Gernika-Lumo* sign), then head up into the hills on BI-635. After visiting Guernica, follow signs along the very twisty BI-2238 road to Lekeitio (about 40 minutes). Leave Lekeitio on the road just above the beach; after crossing the bridge, take the left fork and follow BI-3438 to Markina/Ondarroa (with a striking modern bridge and nice views back into the steep town; follow *portua* signs for free 30-minute parking at the port). Continue to Mutriku and Deba as you hug the coastline east toward San Sebastián. There's a good photo-op pull-out as you climb along the coast just after Deba. Soon after, you'll have two opportunities to get on the AP-8 (blue signs) for a quicker approach to San Sebastián; but if you've enjoyed the scenery so far, stick with the coastal road (white signs, N-634) through Zumaia and Getaria, rejoining the expressway at the high-class resort town of Zarautz.

Lequeitio/Lekeitio

More commonly known by its Euskara name, Lekeitio (leh-KAY-tee-oh)—rather than the Spanish version, Lequeitio—this small

fishing port has an idyllic harbor and a fine beach. It's just over an hour by bus from Bilbao and an easy stop for drivers, and it's protected from the Bay of Biscay by a sand spit that leads to the lush and rugged little San Nicolás Island. Hake boats fly their Basque flags, and proud Basque locals black out the Spanish

translations on street signs.

Lekeitio is a teeming resort during July and August (when its population of 7,000 triples as big-city Basque folks move into their vacation condos). Isolated from the modern rat race by its location down a long, windy little road, it's a backwater fishing village the rest of the year.

Sights here are humble, though the 15th-century St. Mary's Parish Church is a good example of Basque Gothic, with an im-

pressive altarpiece. The town's back lanes are reminiscent of the old days when fishing was the only industry. Fisherwomen sell their husbands' catches each morning along the port. The golden crescent beach is as inviting as the sandbar, which—at low

tide—challenges you to join the seagulls out on San Nicolás Island.

The best beach in the area for surfers and sun lovers is Playas Laga (follow signs off the road from Bilbao to Lekeitio). Relatively uncrowded, it's popular with body-boarders.

Getting There: Bizkaibus #A3523 connects Lekeitio with **Bilbao** (8/day, 1.5 hours; same bus stops at **Guernica**, 40 minutes, https://web.bizkaia.eus). Lurraldebus connects Lekeitio and **San Sebastián** (5/day Mon-Fri, 4/day Sat-Sun, 1.5 hours, www.lurraldebus.eus). But this destination is most logical for those with a car. Drivers can park most easily in the lot near the bus station. Exit the station left, walk along the road, then take the first right (down the steep, cobbled street) to reach the harbor. There is no baggage storage in town.

Tourist Information: The TI faces the fish market next to the harbor (daily 10:00-15:00 & 16:00-19:00, shorter hours and closed Mon Sept-June, +34 946 844 017, www.lekeitio.org).

Eating in Lekeitio: Although it's sleepy off-season, the harbor promenade is made-to-order in summer for a slow meal or a tapas crawl.

Guernica / Gernika

The workaday market town of Guernica (GEHR-nee-kah) is near and dear to Basques and pacifists alike. This is the site of the Gernikako Arbola—the oak tree of Gernika, which marked the assembly point where the regional Basque leaders, the Lords of Bizkaia, met through the ages to assert their people's freedom. Long the symbolic heart of Basque separatism, it was also a natural target for Franco (and Hitler) in the Spanish Civil War—resulting in an infamous bombing raid that left the town in ruins (see "The Bombing of Guernica" sidebar, later), as immortalized by Picasso in his epic work, *Guernica.*

Today's Guernica, rebuilt after being bombed flat in 1937 and nothing special at first glance, holds some of the Basque Country's more compelling museums. And Basque bigwigs have maintained the town as a meeting point—they still elect their figurehead leader on that same ancient site under the oak tree.

Orientation to Guernica

Guernica is small (about 17,000 inhabitants) and compact, focused on its large market hall (Monday market 9:00-14:00).

Tourist Information: The TI is in the town center (Mon-Sat 10:00-19:00, Sun until 14:00, shorter hours in winter, Artekalea 8, +34 946 255 892, http://turismo.gernika-lumo.net). If you'll be visiting both the Peace Museum and the Basque Country Museum, buy the €5 combo-ticket here. Called a "Unified Ticket," it's a great deal but you can only get it at the TI.

Arrival in Guernica: Drivers will find a handy parking lot near the train tracks at the end of town. Buses drop off passengers along the main road skirting the town center. The train station also sits on the main road. No matter how you enter, the TI is well marked (look for yellow *i* signs)—head there first to get your bearings and pick up a handy town map.

Sights in Guernica

I've listed Guernica's sights in the order of a handy sightseeing loop from the TI.

• *Exit the TI to the left, cross the street, and walk up the left side of the square, where you'll find the...*

▲Gernika Peace Museum

Because of the brutality of the Guernica bombing, and the powerful Picasso painting that documented the atrocities of war, the name "Guernica" has become synonymous with pacifism. This thoughtfully presented exhibit has taken a great tragedy of 20th-century history and turned it into a compelling cry for peace in our time.

Cost and Hours: €5, Tue-Sat 10:00-19:00, Sun-Mon until 14:00, closed Mon off-season, Foru Plaza 1, +34 946 270 213, www.museodelapaz.org.

Visiting the Museum: Borrow the English translations at the entry, request an English version of the audio presentation upstairs, and head up through the two-floor exhibit. The first floor begins by considering different ways of defining "peace." You'll then enter an apartment and hear a local woman, Begoña, describe her typical Guernica life in the 1930s...until the bombs dropped (a mirror effect shows you the devastating aftermath). You'll exit through the rubble into an exhibit about the town's history, with a special emphasis on the bombing. Finally, a 10-minute movie shows grainy footage of the destruction and ends with a collage of peaceful reconciliations in recent history—in Ireland, South Africa, Guatemala, Australia, and Berlin. On the second floor, Picasso's famous painting is superimposed on three transparent panels to highlight different themes. The exhibit concludes with a survey of the recent history of conflicts in the Basque Country.

• *Exit left up the stairs and continue uphill to the big church. At the road above the church, you can turn right and walk one block to find a tile replica of Picasso's Guernica (left-hand side of the street). Or you can head left to find the next two attractions.*

▲Basque Country Museum (Euskal Herria Museoa)

This well-presented exhibit offers a good overview of Basque culture and history (though some floors may be closed for restoration). Start in the ground-floor theater (Room 4) and see the overview video (request English). Follow the suggested route and climb

The Bombing of Guernica

During the civil war, Guernica was the site of one of history's most reviled wartime acts.

Monday, April 26, 1937, was market day, when the town was filled with farmers and peasants from the countryside selling their wares. At about 16:40 in the afternoon, a German warplane appeared ominously on the horizon and proceeded to bomb bridges and roads surrounding the town. Soon after, more planes arrived. Three hours of relentless saturation bombing followed, as the German and Italian air forces pummeled the city with incendiary firebombs. People running through the streets or along the green hillsides were strafed with machine-gun fire. As the sun fell low in the sky and the planes finally left, hundreds—or possibly thousands—had been killed, and many more wounded. (Because Guernica was filled with refugees from other besieged towns, nobody is sure how many perished.)

Hearing word of the attack in Paris, Pablo Picasso—who had been commissioned to paint a mural for the 1937 world's fair—was devastated at the news of what had gone on in Guernica. Inspired, he painted what many consider the greatest antiwar work of art, ever.

Why did the bombings happen? Reportedly, Adolf Hitler wanted an opportunity to try out his new saturation-bombing attack strategy. Spanish dictator Francisco Franco, who was fed up with the independence-minded Basques, offered up their historic capital as a candidate for the experiment.

There's no doubt that Guernica, a gateway to Bilbao, was strategically located. And yet, a small munitions factory that supplied anti-Franco forces with pistols oddly wasn't hit by the bombing. Historians believe most of the targets here were far from strategic. Why attack so mercilessly, during the daytime, on market day, when innocent casualties would be maximized? Like the famous silent scream of Picasso's *Guernica* mother, this question haunts pacifists everywhere to this day.

chronologically up through Basque history, with the necessary help of an included audioguide. You'll find exhibits about traditional Basque architecture and landscape, lots of antique maps, and a region-by-region rundown of the Basque Country's seven territories. One interesting map shows Basque emigration over the centuries—including to the US. The top floor is the most engaging, highlighting Basque culture: sports, dances, cuisine, myths and legends, music, and language. For a breath of fresh air, step out back into the **Peoples of Europe Park** and enjoy a peaceful respite.

Cost and Hours: €3.50, free on Sat, includes audioguide except on Sat; open Tue-Sat 10:00-14:00 & 16:00-19:00, Sun 10:30-14:30, closed Mon; Allende Salazar 5, +34 946 255 451.

▲▲Gernika Assembly House and Oak Tree

In the Middle Ages, the meeting point for the Basque general assembly was under the old oak tree on the gentle hillside above Guernica. The tradition continues today, as the tree stands at the center of a modest but interesting complex celebrating Basque culture and self-government.

Cost and Hours: Free, daily 10:00-14:00 & 16:00-19:00, Oct-May until 18:00, on Allende Salazar, +34 946 251 138, www.jjggbizkaia.eus.

Visiting the Assembly House: As you enter the grounds past the guard hut, on the right you'll see an **old tree trunk** in the small colonnade dating from the 1700s. Basque traditions have lived much, much longer than a single tree's life span. When one dies, it's replaced with a new one. This is the oldest surviving trunk.

The exhibit has four parts: a stained-glass window room, the oak-tree courtyard, the assembly chamber, and a basement theater (request the 10-minute video in English that extols the virtues and beauties of the Basque Country).

Inside the main building, pick up a copy of the English brochure that describes in detail the importance of this site. First find the impressive **stained-glass window room.** The computer video here gives a good six-minute overview of the exhibit. The gorgeous stained-glass ceiling is rife with Basque symbolism. The elderly leader stands under the oak holding a book with

the "Old Law" *(Lege Zarra)*, which are the laws by which the Basques lived for centuries. Below him are groups representing the three traditional career groups of this industrious people: sailors and fishermen; miners and steelworkers; and farmers. Behind them all is a classic Basque landscape: On the left is the sea, and on the right are rolling green hills dotted with red-and-white homes. Small, square panels around the large window represent all the important towns in the region, with Guernica's oak tree easy to pinpoint. Step into the wood-paneled library off the main room, and peek into the head honcho's office in the corner.

Out back, a Greek-style tribune surrounds the fateful **oak tree,** a descendant of the nearly century-old ancestor, and possibly of all the trees here since ancient times. This little fella is the fifth tree to stand here—it started growing in 2000 and was planted here in 2015. The previous tree struggled to survive after standing here for just 10 years.

Basque leaders have met in solidarity at this location for centuries. In the Middle Ages, after Basque lands became part of Castile, Castilian kings came here to pledge respect to the old Basque laws. When Basque independence came under fire in the 19th century, patriots rallied by singing a song about this tree ("Ancient and holy symbol / Let thy fruit fall worldwide / While we gaze in adoration / Upon thee, our blessed tree"). After the 1937 bombing, in which this tree's predecessor was miraculously unscathed, hundreds of survivors sought refuge under its branches. Today, although official representatives in the Spanish government are elected at the polls, the Basques choose their figurehead leader, the Lehendakari ("First One"), in this same spot.

Step back inside to enter the **assembly chamber**—like a mini parliament for the region of Bizkaia ("Vizcaya" in Spanish, "Biscay" in English; one of the seven Basque territories). Notice the holy water and the altar—a sign that there was no separation of church and state in Basque politics. The large paintings above the doors show the swearing of allegiance to the Old Law. Portraits of 26 former Lords of Bizkaia maintain a watchful eye over the current assembly's decisions.

• *Exiting the grounds of the Assembly House, walk back to the front of the Basque Country Museum, and take the public school staircase on your right down to Pasealekua Square. At the bottom of the stairs, pop into a café (on your left) known to locals as the...*

Bar de los Jubilados (Old Bomb Shelter)

This unmarked café, part of the retirement community center housed in the same building, is a good place for a quick coffee and snack—but its main claim to fame is that it was a bomb shelter during the 1937 bombing. Ask the bartender, *"¿Dónde está el túnel, por favor?"* You'll be directed toward the women's restroom (gentlemen, don't worry, you can go, too). Walk down the hall, turn right into the women's restroom, and go past the stalls into a small, cold, two-part room. While not much to look at these days, imagine dozens of panicked people scrambling to take shelter here, hoping and praying that they would live through the devastating aerial attack (daily 10:30-21:30, Pasealekua Square).

Guernica Connections

Guernica is well connected to **Bilbao** (2 EuskoTren trains/hour, 50 minutes, arrive at Bilbao's Atxuri station; also 4 buses/hour, 40 minutes) and to **Lekeitio** (8/day, 40 minutes). Connections are sparser on weekends. The easiest way to connect to San Sebastián is via Bilbao, though you can also get there on the slow but scenic "Topo" EuskoTren train (transfer in Lemoa, about 2 hours).

Bilbao / Bilbo

Bilbao (bil-BOW, rhymes with "cow") has seen a transformation like no other Spanish city. Entire sectors of the industrial city's long-depressed port have been cleared away to allow construction of a new convention center, shops, apartment buildings, and the stunning Guggenheim Museum.

Today's Bilbao mingles beautiful old buildings with eyesore high-rise apartment blocks, super-modern additions to the skyline (such as the Guggenheim and its neighbor, the 40-story Iberdrola Tower), and—scattered in the lush hillsides all around the horizon—typical whitewashed Basque homes with red roofs. Bilbao enjoys a vitality and Old World charm befitting its status as a regional capital of culture and industry.

PLANNING YOUR TIME

For most visitors, the Guggenheim is the main draw (and many could spend the entire day there). But with a little more time, it's also worth hopping on a tram to explore the atmospheric old town or a walk along the Nervión River promenade. With even more time, ride the Mount Artxanda funicular for a breathtaking overview of the entire area. Don't bother coming to Bilbao on Monday, when virtually all its museums—including the almighty Guggenheim—are closed (except July-Aug).

Orientation to Bilbao

When you're in the center, Bilbao feels smaller than its population of 350,000. The city, nestled amidst green hillsides, hugs the Nervión River as it curves through town. The Guggenheim is more or less centrally located near the top of that curve; the bus station is to the west; the old town (Casco Viejo) and train stations are to the east; and a super-convenient and fun-to-ride green tram called the EuskoTren Tranbia ties it all together.

SPANISH BASQUE COUNTRY

TOURIST INFORMATION

Bilbao's main TI is housed in a former bank next to the Renfe station at Plaza Circular; look for the red *i* sign above the door (daily 9:00-20:00, +34 944 795 760). If you're interested in something beyond the Guggenheim, ask about their city and themed walking tours in English (described later, under "Tours in Bilbao"). The TI also has a ticket machine for buying EuskoTren tram tickets and the *Barik* public transport card (see "Arrival in Bilbao," below).

Another handy TI is near the main entrance of the Guggenheim; it's a good place to pick up the bimonthly *Bilbao Pocket Guide* (daily 10:00-19:00, off-season Sun until 15:00, Alameda Mazarredo 66, www.bilbaoturismo.net). The Basque Country regional TI office at the airport can help you with information about Bilbao and the entire region (daily 9:00-21:00, +34 944 031 444, www.tourism.euskadi.net).

ARRIVAL IN BILBAO

Most travelers—whether arriving by train, bus, or car—will want to go straight to the Guggenheim. Thanks to a perfectly planned **tram system** (EuskoTren Tranbia), this couldn't be easier. From any point of entry, simply buy a €1.50 single-ride ticket at a user-friendly green machine. If you're planning multiple tram rides or traveling with a small group, consider the *Barik* **public transport card,** which cuts the cost of a single ride to €0.73 (nonrefundable €3 for the card itself, €5 minimum to reload; sold at the airport, Metro stations, the TI on Plaza Circular, kiosks, and the Atxuri EuskoTren train station). *Barik* can be used for up to 10 people riding together on the Metro, buses (including the airport bus), and tram. Activate your

ticket or card at the machine just before boarding (follow the red arrow); you can't do it once on board.

Hop on a green-and-gray tram, enjoy the Muzak, and head for the Guggenheim stop (there's only one line, trams come every 10 minutes). If you get lost, ask: "*¿Dónde está el Guggenheim?*" (DOHN-deh eh-STAH el "Guggenheim"). Note that the only baggage storage in town is at the Intermodal bus station (not at either train station). Don't confuse the green tram with the slow, scenic, blue train to San Sebastián. And while Bilbao has a slick Metro system, most tourists won't need it to get around. Tram info: +34 902 543 210, www.euskotren.eus.

By Train: Bilbao's **Renfe station** (serving most of Spain) is on the river in central Bilbao. The train station is on top of a small shopping mall (a Europcar rental office is upstairs at track level). Unfortunately, the tram stop nearest the train station has no ticket machine and neither does the Renfe station—to board here you'll need to buy a *Barik* card or a single-ride ticket at the TI on Plaza Circular next to the station.

To reach the tram, descend into the stores. Leave from the exit marked *Hurtado de Amézaga* and go right to find the TI and the Abando tram stop. (If the TI is closed, follow the tram tracks across the bridge and around the Arriaga Theater to the next tram stop, Arriaga, where single-ride tickets are sold.) Activate your ticket at the machines at the tram stop before boarding (direction: La Casilla, to reach the Guggenheim).

Trains from San Sebastián arrive at the **Zazpikaleak/Casco Viejo station** in the old town near Plaza Nueva. From here, it's a few minutes' walk to the Arriaga tram stop; buy a ticket before boarding the tram (direction: La Casilla), which follows the river to the Guggenheim stop.

By Bus: Buses stop at the **Intermodal station** (www. bilbaointermodal.eus) on the western edge of downtown, about a mile southwest of the Guggenheim. This new underground station houses a ticket office, WCs, lockers, and a cafeteria. The tram (stop: San Mamés) is on the road by the station —look for the steel *CTB* sign and follow the *EuskoTren* signs (not the escalator that leads to the Metro). Buy and validate a ticket at the machine and hop on the tram (direction: Atxuri) to the Guggenheim or old town.

By Plane: Bilbao's compact, modern, user-friendly airport (airport code: BIO, www.aena.es/en/bilbao-airport) is about six miles north of downtown. Everything branches off the light-and-air-filled main hall, designed by prominent architect Santiago Calatrava. The handy, green Bizkaibus (#3247) takes you directly to the city center—look for a sign outside the far-right exit of the terminal (€3, buy ticket or *Barik* card at the tiny ticket office before boarding, daily 6:15-24:00, 2/hour, 20-minute trip, makes four stops downtown—the first one at Recalde is closest to the Guggenheim—before ending at the Intermodal bus station). A 15-minute taxi ride into town costs about €25. To get to San Sebastián, you can take a direct bus from Bilbao Airport (€17, buy at ticket machine before boarding, runs hourly, 1.5 hours, drops off at Plaza Pío XII in San Sebastián, www.pesa.net). A taxi directly to San Sebastián will run you €150.

By Car: A big underground parking garage is near the museum; if you have a car, park it here and use the tram. From the freeway, take the exit marked *Centro* (with bull's-eye symbol), follow signs to *Guggenheim* (you'll see the museum), and look for the big *P* that marks the garage.

SPANISH BASQUE COUNTRY

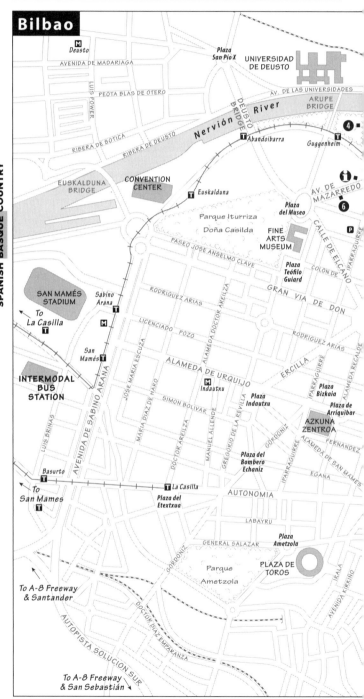

Bilbao

Accommodations
1. Gran Hotel Domine Bilbao
2. Hotel Bilbao Plaza

Eateries
3. Nerua
4. Outdoor Café

5. Nostrum
6. La Casa del Bacalao
7. Bar Ledesma
8. Café Iruña

SPANISH BASQUE COUNTRY

To Airport

AV. DE MAURICE RAVEL

LA SALVE BRIDGE
GUGGENHEIM BILBAO
PUPPY

Plaza de la Salve
CASTAÑOS
HUERTAS DE LA VILLA
EPALZA
ARTXANDA FUNICULAR STATION

PASEO CAMPO DE VOLANTÍN

LERSUNDI
LOS HEROS
HENAO
ERCILLA
LARREATEGUI
Plaza Moyúa
DIEGO LOPEZ DE HARO
Moyúa
CALLE DE ELCANO
E. CAMPO
Plaza Zabálburu
GEN. CONCHA
CALLE DE URQUIJO

ALAMEDA DE MAZARREDO
URIBITARTE
IBAÑEZ DE BILBAO
COLÓN DE LARREATEGUI
CALLE LEDESMA
Plaza Circular
Abando
ALAMEDA DE AMEZAGA
HURTADO DE AMEZAGA
JUAN DE GARCIA SALAZAR
BAILEN
SAN FRANCISCO

Uribitarte
ZUBIZURI BRIDGE
BILBOATS
Plaza Pío Baroja
Plaza San Vicente
SAN VICENTE MÁRTIR
Pío Baroja
BUENOS AIRES
Abando

TIBOLI
MATIKO
URIBARRI

Parque Etxebarria

AYUNTAMIENTO
Pío Baroja
AYUNTAMIENTO BRIDGE

Nervión River

ZAZPIKALEAK/ CASCO VIEJO EUSKOTREN STATION

ARENAL BRIDGE
ARRIAGA THEATER
Arriaga
Plaza Nueva

RENFE TRAIN STATION (ABANDO)

OLD TOWN

PERRO
BASQUE MUSEUM

CALLE DE LA RIBERA

SANTIAGO CATHEDRAL
Ribera

LA RIBERA MARKET
SAN ANTÓN
Atxuri

ATXURI TRAIN STATION

MUSEUM OF SACRED ART

See Old Town detail map

To A-8 Freeway & San Sebastián

200 Meters
200 Yards

To Guernica

HELPFUL HINTS

Sightseeing Cards: The **Bilbao Bizkaia Card** is sold at TIs and online (www.bilbaobizkaiacard.com). It covers transportation, including the Artxanda funicular, and two TI walking tours, plus allows you to skip the line when buying tickets at the Guggenheim and the Fine Arts Museum (€10/24 hours, €15/48 hours, €20/72 hours). If you're only visiting the Guggenheim and Fine Arts Museum, consider the **Artean Pass** combo-ticket (see museum listings for details).

Baggage Storage: The Intermodal bus station on the west side of the city is your best option (Gurtubay 1, +34 944 395 077).

Laundry: The self-service **Lavandería Autoservicio Adei** is handy for visitors staying in the old town. You don't even have to buy detergent—it's already dispensed in the machines (daily 8:00-22:00, last load at 21:00, Ribera 9, mobile +34 665 710 082).

Tours in Bilbao

Walking Tours

Bilbao Walking Tours offers 1.5-hour tours on Saturdays and Sundays (more often in summer), including an old-town tour at 10:00 and a modern-city tour at 12:00 showing the city's history since the 19th century (both start at the Plaza Circular TI). Tours are in Spanish and English, and it's best to reserve in advance. The walks are timed so that you can do both in a single day (€4.50, free with Bilbao Bizkaia Card, +34 944 795 760, www.bilbaoturismo.net, informacion@bilbaoturismo.bilbao.eus).

Tram Tour

Riding the EuskoTren round-trip between the Atxuri and Euskalduna stops is a great way to see the city's oldest and newest neighborhoods, especially on rainy days. For more on this tram, see "Arrival in Bilbao," earlier.

Boat Tour

For a different view of the city, try the **Bilboats** one-hour tour along the river, offering plenty of architectural photo ops. The tour begins near Ayuntamiento Bridge (€13, daily in spring and summer at 13:00, 16:00, 17:30, and 19:00, fewer departures off-season; reserve ahead, trips are canceled if fewer than 10 people buy tickets; tram stop: Pío Baroja; Plaza de Pío Baroja, +34 946 424 157, www.bilboats.com). For hardcore sailors, a two-hour version goes all the way to the Bay of Biscay, passing under the unique suspension bridge in Portugalete (€19, daily July-Aug at 10:30, Thu-Sun only rest of year).

Bike Tour

Although Bilbao is not the most bike-friendly city, bike lanes close to both sides of the Nervión River offer a pleasant ride. At **Tourné Bilbao,** you can rent bikes (€8/2 hours, €10/4 hours) or join their city bike tour, which starts daily at 10:30 with a *pintxo* included (€32/3 hours, near the Renfe station and TI at Villarías Kalea 1, +34 944 249 465, www.tournebilbao.com, info@tournebilbao.com).

Local Guide

Knowledgeable Bilbao resident and licensed guide **Iratxe Muñoz** offers tours of the city, including the Guggenheim and the Basque region (rates vary, mobile +34 607 778 072, iratxe.m@apite.eu).

Sights in Bilbao

▲▲▲Guggenheim Bilbao

Although the collection of art in this museum is no better than those in Europe's other great modern-art museums, the build-

ing itself—designed by Frank Gehry and opened in 1997—is reason enough for many travelers to happily splice Bilbao into their itineraries. Even if you're not turned on by contemporary art, the Guggenheim is a must-see experience. Its 20 galleries, on three floors, are full of surprises, and it's well worth the entry fee just to appreciate the museum's structural design, which is a masterpiece in itself.

Cost and Hours: €13 online in advance, €15 onsite, both prices include audioguide; €20 Artean Pass also covers Fine Arts Museum (but does not include the Guggenheim's €2 audioguide); Tue-Sun 10:00-20:00, closed Mon except in July-Aug; same-day re-entry allowed—get wristband on your way out; café; tram stop: Guggenheim, Avenida Abandoibarra 2, +34 944 359 080, www.guggenheim-bilbao.eus.

Tours: A free and excellent audioguide is included with a regular entry ticket. Depending on demand, the museum offers two guided tours in English: a 30-minute tour describing the art on exhibit (Mon-Fri at 17:00, Sat-Sun at 12:30), and a 60-minute tour providing an overview of the building and institution (Mon-Fri at 12:30, Sat-Sun at 17:00). Show up at least 30 minutes early to put your name on the list at the information desk (to the left as you enter). Private guided 1.5-hour tours in English are available by advance reservation (€125 in addition to admission fee, call from

9:00-14:00 to book, mobile +34 647 574 026, guidedtoursmgb@ eulen.com).

Background: Frank Gehry's groundbreaking triumph offers a fascinating look at 21st-century architecture. Using cutting-edge technologies, unusual materials, and daring forms, he created a piece of sculpture that smoothly integrates with its environment and serves as the perfect stage for some of today's best art. Clad in limestone and titanium, the building connects the city with its river. Gehry meshed many visions. To him, the building's multiple forms jostle like a loose crate of bottles. The building is inspired by a silvery fish...and also evokes wind-filled sails heading out to sea. Gehry keeps returning to his fish motif, reminding visitors that, as a boy, he was inspired by carp...even taking them into the bathtub with him.

Visiting the Museum: The audioguide will lead you room-by-room through the collection, but this information will get you started.

Guarding the main entrance is artist Jeff Koons' 42-foot-tall **West Highland Terrier.** Its 60,000 plants and flowers, which blossom in concert, grow through steel mesh. A joyful structure, it brings viewers back to their childhoods—perhaps evoking human-kind's relationship to God—or maybe it's just another notorious Koons hoax. One thing is clear: It answers to "Puppy." Although the sculpture was originally intended to be temporary, the people of Bilbao fell in love with *Puppy*—so they bought it.

Descend to the **main entrance,** where you can show or buy your ticket and collect the audioguide. At the information desk, pick up the small English brochure explaining the architecture and museum layout, and the seasonal *Guggenheim Bilbao* magazine that details the art currently on display.

Enter the **atrium.** This acts as the heart of the building, pumping visitors from various rooms on three levels out and back, always returning to this central area before moving on to the next. The architect invites you to caress the sensual curves of the walls. There are virtually no straight lines (except the floor). Notice the sheets of glass that make up the staircase and elevator shafts—overlapping each other like a fish's scales. Each glass and limestone panel is unique, designed by a computer and shaped by a robot...as will likely be standard in constructing the great buildings of the future.

From the atrium, step out onto the riverside **terrace.** The "water garden" lets the river symbolically lap at the base of the building. This pool is home to four unusual sculptures (the first two appear occasionally throughout the day): Yves Klein's five-part "fire fountain" (notice the squares in the pool to the right); Fujiko Nakaya's "fog sculpture" that billows up from below; another piece by Jeff Koons, *Tulips,* which is a colorful chrome bouquet of inflated flowers; and the most recent addition, *Tall Tree and the Eye* by British artist Anish Kapoor. Composed of 73 reflective spheres arranged vertically, the sculpture endlessly reflects the Guggenheim, the river, and the beholder.

Still out on the terrace, notice the museum's commitment to public spaces: On the right, a grand **staircase** leads under a big green bridge to a tower; the effect wraps the bridge into the museum's grand scheme. The 30-foot-tall **spider,** called *Maman* ("Mommy"), is French American artist Louise Bourgeois' depiction of her mother: She spins a beautiful and delicate web of life... which is used to entrap her victims. (It makes a little more sense if you understand that the artist's mother was a weaver. Or maybe not.)

Step back inside. Gehry designed the vast **ground floor** mainly to house often-huge modern-art installations. Computer-controlled lighting adjusts for different exhibits. Surfaces are clean and bare, so you can focus on the art. While most of the collection comes and goes, Richard Serra's huge *Matter of Time* sculpture in the largest gallery (#104) is permanent. Who would want to move those massive metal coils? The intent is to have visitors walk among these metal walls—the "art" is experiencing this journey.

Because this museum is part of the Guggenheim "family" of museums, the **collection** perpetually rotates among the sister Guggenheim galleries in New York and Venice. The best approach to your visit is simply to immerse yourself in a modern-art happening, rather than to count on seeing a particular piece or a specific artist's works.

You can't fully enjoy the museum's architecture without taking a circular stroll up and down each side of the river along the handsome promenade and over the two modern **pedestrian bridges.** (After you tour the museum, you can borrow a free "outdoor audioguide" to learn more—ID required—but it doesn't say much or take you across the river.) The building's skin—shiny and metallic, with a scale-like texture—is made of thin titanium, carefully created to give just the desired color and reflective quality. The external appearance tells you what's inside: The blocky limestone parts contain square-shaped galleries, and the titanium sections hold nonlinear spaces.

As you look out over the rest of the city, think of this: Gehry designed his building to reflect what he saw here in Bilbao. Now other architects are, in turn, creating new buildings that complement his. It's an appealing synergy for this old city.

Leaving the Museum: To get to the old town from the Guggenheim, you can take the tram that leaves from the river level beside the museum, just past the kid-pleasing fountain (ride it in direction: Atxuri). Hop off at the Arriaga stop, near the dripping-

SPANISH BASQUE COUNTRY

Baroque riverfront theater of the same name. From here, cross the street to enter the heart of the old town.

Or, for a pleasant 20-minute walk, exit the museum and go behind it to the river. Head toward the spider *Maman,* passing under her and the tall bridge *La Salve,* which is incorporated into the museum. Continue along the river, passing the white, harp-shaped Santiago Calatrava bridge *(Zubizuri),* a second bridge *(Ayuntamiento),* and finally crossing at the third bridge *(Arenal)* to arrive at the old town. (Bridges are labeled on city maps.)

NEAR THE GUGGENHEIM
Fine Arts Museum (Museo de Bellas Artes)

Often overshadowed by the Guggenheim, the Fine Arts Museum contains a thoughtfully laid out collection arranged chronologically from the 12th century to the present. Find minor works by many Spanish artists, such as Goya, El Greco, Picasso, Murillo, Zurbarán, Sorolla, Chillida, Tàpies, and Barceló—along with a handful of local Basque painters. Other international artists in the collection include Gauguin, Klee, Bacon, Cassatt, and more. The museum is at the edge of the lovely Doña Casilda Iturrizar Park, perfect for a stroll after your visit.

Cost and Hours: €10, includes audioguide; free after 18:00 when the audioguide is €3; €20 Artean Pass also covers the Guggenheim (includes Fine Arts Museum audioguide and temporary exhibits); Wed-Mon 10:00-20:00, closed Tue; a short walk from the Guggenheim at Museo Plaza 2, +34 944 396 060, www.museobilbao.com.

Azkuna Zentroa (Alhóndiga Bilbao)

Bilbao's culture and leisure center, designed by French architect Philippe Starck, is worth a quick visit or a lazy afternoon. Not one of the 43 interior columns is alike—the designs are meant to represent the entirety of materials and styles from antiquity to today. The center houses a cinema, auditorium, exhibition spaces, and restaurant—so it functions as a community gathering space. Most impressive is its glass-bottomed rooftop pool—from the atrium below, visitors can gaze up at the backstrokers in the water above.

Cost and Hours: Free entry to the center itself, €7 day pass gives you access to the pool and sundeck, daily 8:30-23:00, 10-minute walk from the Guggenheim at Plaza Arriquibar 4, +34 944 014 014, www.azkunazentroa.eus.

Funicular de Artxanda

Opened in 1915, this funicular still provides *bilbainos* with a green escape from their somewhat grimy city. The three-minute ride offers sweeping views of the city on the way to the top of Mount Artxanda, where there's a park, restaurants, and a sports complex.

Bring a picnic on a sunny afternoon, and take a moment to ponder the giant thumbprint sculpture dedicated to Basque soldiers who fought against Franco during the civil war.

Cost and Hours: €4.30 round-trip, covered by the Bilbao Bizkaia Card; leaves every 15 minutes, daily 7:15-22:00, until 23:00 in summer; cross the Zubizuri Bridge and walk two blocks along Calle Mújica y Burton to the cable-car station, Plaza del Funicular, +34 944 454 966.

IN THE OLD TOWN

Bilbao's old town (Casco Viejo), with tall, narrow lanes lined with thriving shops and tapas bars, is worth a stroll. Because the weather is wetter here than in many other parts of Spain (hence the green hillsides), the little balconies that climb the outside walls of buildings are glassed in, creating cozy little breakfast nooks.

Whether you want to or not, you'll eventually wind up at Old Bilbao's centerpiece, the **Santiago Cathedral,** a 14th-century Gothic church with a tranquil interior that has been scrubbed clean inside and out (€5 combo-ticket includes audioguide and entrance to the San Anton Church next to La Ribera Market, daily July-Aug 10:00-21:00, Sept-June until 20:00, Plaza Santiago 1, +34 944 153 627, www.catedralbilbao.com).

Various museums (including those dedicated to diocesan art and the Holy Week processions) are in or near the old town, but on a quick visit only one is worth considering...

Basque Museum (Euskal Museoa)

As a leading city of Spain's Basque region, Bilbao has lovingly assembled artifacts of Basque heritage in this 16th-century convent. English pamphlets scattered throughout offer helpful summaries of the displays.

Cost and Hours: €3, Mon and Wed-Fri 10:00-19:00, Sat 10:00-13:30 & 16:00-19:00, Sun 10:00-14:00, closed Tue, Miguel de Unamuno Plaza 4, +34 944 155 423, http://www.euskal-museoa.eus.

Visiting the Museum: For the most part, follow the museum's standard route.

The main sight in the ground-floor cloister is the Iron-Age *El Mikeldi,* a stone animal figure. The first floor centers on the maritime activities of the seafaring Basques, as well as the pastoral lifestyle of the region's shepherds. The second floor has exhibits covering porcelain, timeworn tools, and ironworks that helped spur the economic prominence of the Basque region.

On the top floor are fragments from two oak trees from Guernica—cherished relics of Basque nationalism (see the Guernica section, earlier). The Arbol Viejo and the Arbol Nuevo each stood for 150 years in front of the Gernika Assembly House until their "clinical death." This floor also has exhibits on the social, political, and economic impact of Bilbao over three centuries.

La Ribera Market

With a three-star Michelin restaurant, Bilbao seems poised to give San Sebastián a run for its money as culinary capital of the Basque Country. As part of an urban renewal plan, the 1929 La Ribera city market reopened in 2011 to an enthusiastic public. Stroll the stalls for the freshest fish (look for the busiest sellers), shop for produce, and admire a series of Art Deco stained-glass panels on the top floor. The city's coat-of-arms, with two wolves, can be found in the largest panels. There's been a market here since Bilbao was founded in 1300. Consider returning in the afternoon or evening to the stylish *cervecería* and the few *pintxo* bars on the ground floor (Mon-Sat 8:00-14:30, also Tue-Fri 17:00-20:00, closed Sun, public WCs, +34 946 023 791).

Sleeping in Bilbao

Bilbao merits an overnight stay. Even those who are interested only in the Guggenheim find that there's much more to see in this historic yet quickly changing city.

NEAR THE GUGGENHEIM MUSEUM

For locations, see the "Bilbao" map on page 46.

$$$$ Gran Hotel Domine Bilbao is *the* place for well-heeled modern-art fans looking for a splurge close to the museum. It's right across the street from the main entrance to the Guggenheim and Jeff Koons' *Puppy*. The hotel is gathered around an atrium with a giant "stone tree" and other artsy flourishes, and its decor (by a prominent Spanish designer) was clearly inspired by Gehry's masterpiece. The 145 plush rooms are distinctly black, white, steel, and very postmodern (air-con, elevator, free gym with wet and dry saunas, pay parking, Alameda Mazarredo 61, +34 944 253 300, www.hoteldominebilbao.com, info@hoteldominebilbao.com). Breakfast on the hotel's great museum-view terrace is a treat open even to nonguests (served daily 7:00-11:00, Sat-Sun until 12:00). If arriving by tram, take the main museum steps up by the fountains to reach the hotel.

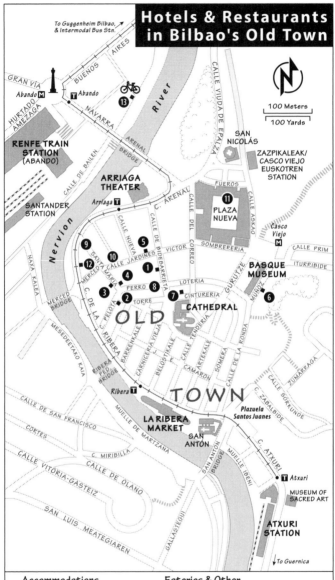

Hotels & Restaurants in Bilbao's Old Town

To Guggenheim Bilbao, & Intermodal Bus Stn.

100 Meters
100 Yards

SPANISH BASQUE COUNTRY

RENFE TRAIN STATION (ABANDO)

SANTANDER STATION

ARRIAGA THEATER

SAN NICOLÁS

ZAZPIKALEAK/ CASCO VIEJO EUSKOTREN STATION

PLAZA NUEVA

Casco Viejo M

BASQUE MUSEUM

CATHEDRAL

O L D

T O W N

Nervión

LA RIBERA MARKET

SAN ANTÓN

Plazuela Santos Juanes

MUSEUM OF SACRED ART

ATXURI STATION

To Guernica

Accommodations
1. Casual Gurea Bilbao
2. Basque Boutique
3. Iturrienea Ostatua
4. 7Kale Bed & Breakfast; Pensión Mendez
5. Hotel Bilbao Jardines
6. La Estrella Ostatu

Eateries & Other
7. Baster
8. Calle del Perro Eateries
9. Calle Santa María Eateries
10. Calle Jardines Eateries
11. Plaza Nueva Eateries
12. Launderette
13. Bike Rental

$$ Hotel Bilbao Plaza has 53 bright and modern rooms, pleasant public spaces, and a friendly staff. With a great location on the river, it's a 10-minute walk to the Guggenheim and a five-minute walk to modern Bilbao or the edge of the old town—so it's away from the bar noise at night (air-con, elevator, pay parking, Paseo Campo Volantín 1, at the Ayuntamiento bridge, +34 946 856 700, www.hotelbilbaoplaza.com, info@hotelbilbaoplaza.com).

IN AND NEAR THE OLD TOWN
To reach the old town, take the tram to the Arriaga stop.

$$ Casual Gurea Bilbao has 26 clean, well-priced rooms and a welcoming staff. Double-pane windows make the rooms quiet despite being on a busy street. There's a common area with coffee and vending machines (elevator, Calle Bidebarrieta 14, third floor, +34 944 163 299, www.casualgurea.com, gurea@casualhoteles.com).

$$ Basque Boutique offers eight classy rooms with petite balconies. All rooms are designed with Basque themes, such as the "El Caserío" room with traditional Basque furniture and the "Gernika" room inspired by the painting by Pablo Picasso. The shared space has free coffee and tea, and you can try on traditional Basque clothing to take a fun photo (air-con, no elevator, Calle de la Torre 2, second floor, +34 944 790 788, www.basqueboutique.es, info@basqueboutique.es).

$$ Iturrienea Ostatua is a polished, quaint version of a traditional *pensión* with nine rooms, a breakfast room, rustic decor, and mini fridges. Double-pane windows help with the noise, but if you are sensitive, bring earplugs or ask for an interior room (Calle Santa María 14, first floor, +34 944 161 500, www.iturrieneaostatua.com, iturrienea@outlook.es).

$ 7Kale Bed & Breakfast, across the street from Iturrienea Ostatua, has a similar concept. They have 12 bright rooms with private bathrooms, and a small breakfast room. Balcony rooms are lovely, but the hotel is on a pedestrian street that's lively at night and can be noisy—ask for a quiet room away from the street (Calle Santa María 13, first floor, +34 946 402 011, www.7kalebnb.com, 7kale@7kalebnb.com).

$ Hotel Bilbao Jardines is a slumbermill buried in the old town with 32 modern but basic rooms and squeaky floors (air-con, elevator, free loaner bicycles, Calle Jardines 9, +34 944 794 210, www.hotelbilbaojardines.com, info@hotelbilbaojardines.com; Marta, Félix, and Mónica).

$ La Estrella Ostatu is a family-run establishment with 26 simple but neat rooms up a twisty staircase near the Basque Museum. It's on a busy pedestrian street with several bars—bring earplugs (María Muñoz 6, +34 944 164 066, www.la-estrella-ostatu.

com, laestrellabilbao@yahoo.es, just enough English spoken, Jesus and Begoña).

¢ **Pensión Mendez** provides basic old-school *pensión* accommodations, with shared bathrooms and stoic but professional service (Calle Santa María 13, fourth floor, +34 944 160 364, www.pensionmendez.com, comercial@pensionmendez.com).

Eating in Bilbao

Bilbao has a thriving restaurant and tapas-bar scene. For pointers on Basque food, see "Basque Country Cuisine Scene" section, earlier. While each neighborhood has a clustering of bars and restaurants, the best spots are in the old town, and in the new town area between the Guggenheim and old town. The area around the Guggenheim also has several good options.

NEAR THE GUGGENHEIM MUSEUM

The easiest choice is the good **$$$ bar** in the museum itself, which features *pintxos,* salads, and sandwiches (upper level, separate entry above museum entry; Tue-Sun 9:30-20:30, also open Mon July-Aug). Adjacent to the bar is the museum's more chic **$$$ Bistro,** with an express lunch (reservations smart, fixed-price meal offered all day, open for dinner Thu-Sat, +34 944 239 333, www.bistroguggenheimbilbao.com). The finest dining experience is at the one-Michelin-star restaurant **$$$$ Nerua,** with waiters almost as fancy as the food (riverfront access upstairs outside museum, Tue-Sun 13:00-15:00, evening service Thu-Sat 20:30-22:00, closed Mon, +34 944 000 430, www.neruaguggenheimbilbao.com).

The circular structure outside the museum by the playgrounds and fountains is a pleasant **outdoor café** serving sandwiches. If the tables are full, you can take your food to one of the stone benches nearby. In the evenings, they sometimes have live music.

The streets in front of the museum have a handful of **$** sit-down and takeout eateries (cafés, pizzerias, sandwich shops). Two places to consider are **Nostrum,** which has packaged salads, pastas, and more—perfect for a picnic in front of the Guggenheim or to heat and eat at their handful of tables (Iparraguirre 1, Mon-Fri 9:00-20:00, Sat from 10:00, closed Sun) and **La Casa del Bacalao,** where the food is heartier, more local, and homemade (food can be heated, but there are no tables; Mon-Fri 10:30-16:00 & 18:00-21:00, Sat 10:30-15:00, Sun 11:00-15:00; Alameda Mazarredo 79, +34 946 853 145). For locations, see the "Bilbao" map on page 46.

IN THE OLD TOWN

You'll find plenty of options on the lanes near the cathedral or on Plaza Nueva. Most restaurants around the old town advertise a fixed-price lunch for around €13; some close for siesta between 16:00 and 20:00. For locations see the "Hotels & Restaurants in Bilbao's Old Town" map.

Calle Correo: The hip little bar **$$ Baster** is just behind the cathedral. Sit in the small interior or delightful outdoor seating for late breakfast, *pintxos,* their well-known *patatas bravas,* or fresh *tortillas de patas.* They also have a good selection of vermouth and craft beers (Tue-Thu 9:30-22:00, Fri-Sat until 23:00, Sun until 16:00, closed Mon, Calle Correo 22, +34 944 071 228).

Calle del Perro: This street is tops for tasty *pintxos.* **$$ Xukela Bar** is my favorite, with its inviting atmosphere, good wines, and an addictive array of tapas spread along its bar. The adventurous might try their specialty—*cresta de gallo,* a.k.a. fried rooster comb (tables generally only for clients eating hot dishes, Calle del Perro 2, +34 944 159 772). Calle del Perro is also good for sit-down restaurants. Browse the menus and interiors and choose your favorite. Well-regarded options include three **$$** places virtually next door to each other: **Egiluz** (meals served in small restaurant up steep spiral staircase in the back); **Río-Oja** (focus on shareable traditional dishes called *cazuelitas*); and **Rotterdam** (also has *cazuelitas* displayed on the bar; try the *chipirones en su tinta*—squids in their own ink). Across from Río-Oja, **$$ Restaurante Mandoya** is a charming sit-down place with a friendly staff and appealing interior. They specialize in both fish and meat, serving up hearty lunch portions. It gets busy, so come early or make a reservation (Tue-Sun 13:30-15:30, Fri-Sat also open 21:00-23:30, closed Mon, Calle del Perro 3, +34 944 157 984, www.restaurantemandoya.com).

Calle Santa María: This street caters to a younger crowd, with softer lighting and a livelier atmosphere, and has several bars and restaurants worth considering: Gatz, Santa María, Kasko, Con B de Bilbao, and Amarena. **$$$ Kasko** is a good sit-down option, with a pianist and an interesting fixed-price lunch and dinner (daily, Santa María 16, +34 944 160 311). **$$ Con B de Bilbao** serves beautiful and hearty *pintxos* or *montaditos* in a trendy, eclectic setting (closed Sun for dinner, Calle Santa María 9, +34 944 158 776). Busy **$$ Amarena** is probably the best choice if you want a full restaurant meal (daily, on the corner at Calle Santa María 18, +34 944 169 421).

Calle Jardines: Eateries also abound on Jardines street, including the popular **$$ Berton** and its sister bar/dining room **$$ Berton Sasibil,** across the lane (at #11 and #8, closed Mon, +34 944 167 035). **$ Charamel Gozotegia** has coffee, tea, and pastry to follow your *pintxo* lunch. Ask for the traditional *pastel vasco*

(Basque cake) or their specialty *milhoja artesana* (Napoleon), all homemade by a group of young, creative bakers (daily until 20:30, Calle Jardines 2, +34 944 165 984).

Plaza Nueva and Calle del Arenal: The old town's living room, Plaza Nueva is full of outdoor café tables, lively *pintxo* bars, kids playing ball, and a stamp, coin, and used-book market on Sunday morning. It's a great local scene to take in. For good *pintxos*, check out the award-winning **$$ Gure Toki** and its neighbor bar **$$ Sorginzulo,** both with outdoor seating.

IN THE NEW TOWN

You'll see cafés, restaurants, and *pintxo* bars scattered along the way from the Guggenheim to the old town in the neighborhood parallel to the Nervión River. The most concentrated and accessible area is on and near the pedestrian street Calle Ledesma, which runs parallel to Gran Vía de Don Diego López de Haro. On a busy night, you won't be able to tell where people ordered their drinks as they flow up and down the street. The classic **$$ Bar Ledesma,** at #14, draws a crowd, but most of the places on this strip have similar *pintxos* and drinks. Around the corner, on the large inviting square called Jardines de Albia, is **$$ Café Iruña,** a café-bar-restaurant with Andalusian decor serving breakfast as well as *pintxos* and full meals (fixed-price weekday meal, long hours daily, +34 944 237 021). For locations see the "Bilbao" map on page 46.

Bilbao Connections

From Bilbao by Bus to: San Sebastián (2/hour, hourly on weekends, 1.5 hours), **Guernica** (4/hour, fewer on weekends, 40 minutes), **Lekeitio** (hourly, 1.5 hours), **Pamplona** (6/day, 2 hours), **Burgos** (8/day, fewer on weekends, 2-3 hours), **Santander** (hourly, 1.5 hours, transfer there to bus to **Santillana del Mar** or **Comillas**). These buses depart from Bilbao's Intermodal station (tram stop: San Mamés, www.bilbaointermodal.eus).

By Renfe Train to: Madrid (2/day direct, more with transfer, 5-7 hours), **Barcelona** (2/day, 7 hours), **Burgos** (3/day direct, more with transfer, 3 hours), **Salamanca** (3/day, 6 hours), **León** (2/day, 5 hours). Remember, these trains leave from the Renfe station, across the river from the old town (tram stop: Abando).

By EuskoTren to: San Sebastián (hourly, long and scenic 2.5-hour trip to San Sebastián's Amara EuskoTren station, departs from Bilbao's Zazpikaleak/Casco Viejo station just east of Plaza Nueva), **Guernica** (2/hour, 50 minutes, take Bilbao-Bermeo line from Atxuri station, just beyond the Ribera Market, direction: Bermeo). EuskoTren info: www.euskotren.eus.

Pamplona

Proud Pamplona, with stout old walls standing guard in the Pyrenees foothills, is the capital of the province of Navarre ("Navarra" in Spanish). At its peak in the Middle Ages, Navarre was a grand kingdom that controlled parts of today's Spain and France. (The king of Spain, Felipe VI, is a descendant of the French line of Navarre royalty.) After the French and Spanish parts split, Pamplona remained the capital of Spanish Navarre.

Today Pamplona—called "Iruña" in the Basque language—feels at once affluent (with the sleek new infrastructure of a town on the rise), claustrophobic (with its warren of narrow lanes), and fascinating (with its odd traditions, rich history, and ties to Hemingway). Culturally, the city is a lively hodgepodge of Basque and Navarro. Locals like to distinguish between Vascos (people of Basque citizenship—not them) and Vascones (people who identify culturally as Basques—as do many Navarros). Pamplona is also an important seat for a controversial wing of the Catholic Church, Opus Dei, founded in Spain in 1928 by the Catholic priest Josemaría Escrivá. He established the private Pamplona-based University of Navarra, and Opus Dei also runs a hospital and several schools in the city.

Of course, Pamplona is best known as the host of one of Spain's (and Europe's) most famous festivals: the Running of the Bulls (held in conjunction with the Fiesta de San Fermín, July 6-14). For latecomers, San Fermín Txikito ("Little San Fermín") offers a less touristy alternative in late September. But there's more to this town than bulls—and, in fact, visiting at other times is preferable to the crowds and 24/7 party atmosphere that seize Pamplona during the festival. Contrary to the chaotic or even backward image that its famous festival might suggest, Pamplona generally feels welcoming, sane, and enjoyable.

Orientation to Pamplona

Pamplona has about 200,000 people. Most everything of interest is in the tight, twisting lanes of the old town *(casco antiguo)*, centered on the main square, Plaza del Castillo. The newer Ensanche ("Expansion") neighborhood just to the south—with a sensible grid plan—holds several good hotels and the bus station.

TOURIST INFORMATION

Pamplona's TI is located next to City Hall (daily 9:00-14:00 & 15:00-20:00, shorter hours off-season, on Plaza Consistorial at Calle San Saturnino 2, +34 948 420 700, www.pamplona.es).

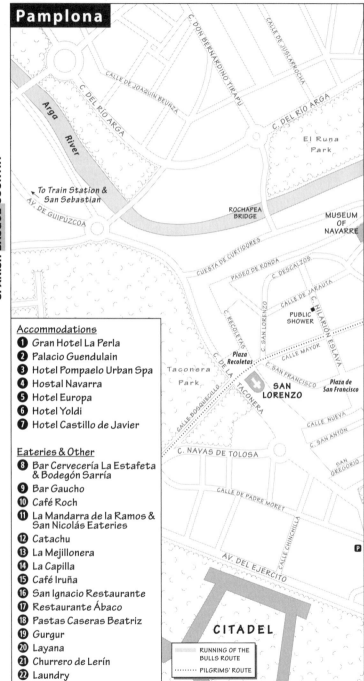

SPANISH BASQUE COUNTRY

Pamplona

Arga River

CALLE DE JOAQUIN BEUNZA

C. DEL RÍO ARGA

C. DON BERNARDINO TIRAPU

CALLE DE JUSLARROCHA

C. DEL RÍO ARGA

El Runa Park

To Train Station & San Sebastian

AV. DE GUIPÚZCOA

ROCHAPEA BRIDGE

MUSEUM OF NAVARRE

CUESTA DE CURTIDORES

PASEO DE RONDA

C. DESCALZOS

CALLE DE JARAUTA

C. HILARIÓN ESLAVA

PUBLIC SHOWER

C. SAN LORENZO

C. RECOLETAS

CALLE MAYOR

Plaza Recoletas

Taconera Park

C. DE LA TACONERA

CALLE BOGUECILLO

C. SAN FRANCISCO

SAN LORENZO

Plaza de San Francisco

CALLE NUEVA

C. SAN ANTÓN

C. NAVAS DE TOLOSA

SAN GREGORIO

CALLE DE PADRE MORET

CALLE CHINCHILLA

AV. DEL EJÉRCITO

CITADEL

Accommodations

1. Gran Hotel La Perla
2. Palacio Guendulain
3. Hotel Pompaelo Urban Spa
4. Hostal Navarra
5. Hotel Europa
6. Hotel Yoldi
7. Hotel Castillo de Javier

Eateries & Other

8. Bar Cervecería La Estafeta & Bodegón Sarría
9. Bar Gaucho
10. Café Roch
11. La Mandarra de la Ramos & San Nicolás Eateries
12. Catachu
13. La Mejillonera
14. La Capilla
15. Café Iruña
16. San Ignacio Restaurante
17. Restaurante Ábaco
18. Pastas Caseras Beatriz
19. Gurgur
20. Layana
21. Churrero de Lerín
22. Laundry

RUNNING OF THE BULLS ROUTE
········ PILGRIMS' ROUTE

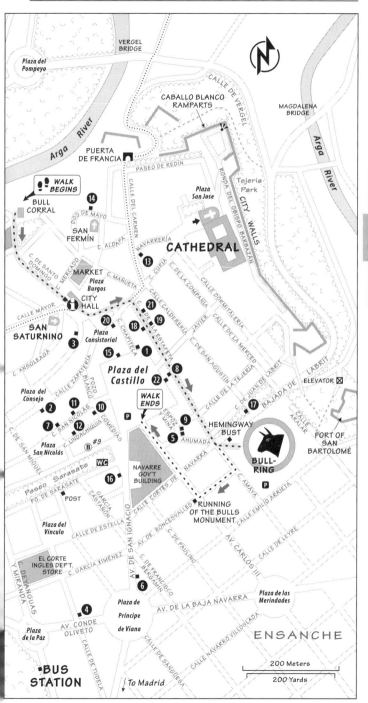

SPANISH BASQUE COUNTRY

ARRIVAL IN PAMPLONA

You can store bags at the bus station, but not at the train station.

By Bus: The sleek, user-friendly bus station is underground along the western edge of the Ensanche area at Calle Yanguas y Miranda 2, about a 10-minute walk from the old-town sightseeing zone. The station has a multilingual information desk that makes trip planning a breeze (Mon-Fri 10:00-14:00 & 15:00-19:00, Sat-Sun 10:00-13:00 & 16:00-19:00, +34 948 203 566). On arrival, go up the escalators, cross the street, turn left, and walk a half-block, where you can turn right down the busy Conde Oliveto street. Along this street, you're near several of my recommended accommodations—or you can walk two blocks to the big traffic circle called Plaza Príncipe de Viana. From here, turn left up Avenida de San Ignacio to reach the old town.

By Train: The Renfe station is farther from the center, across the river to the northwest. It's easiest to hop on public bus #9 (€1.35, every 15 minutes), which stops at the big Plaza Príncipe de Viana traffic circle south of the old town—look for a roundabout with a fountain in the center—as well as Paseo de Sarasate near Plaza del Castillo.

By Car: Everything is well marked: Simply follow the bull's-eyes to the center of town, where individual hotels are clearly signposted. There's also handy parking right at Plaza del Castillo and Plaza de Toros, where the bullring is (close to several recommended hotels).

By Plane: Pamplona Airport is located about four miles outside the city (code: PNA, +34 913 211 000, www.aena.es). A taxi from the airport to the city center costs around €12.

HELPFUL HINTS

No Bull—There's Another Fiesta: The last weekend in September, Pamplona celebrates **San Fermín Txikito** ("Little San Fermín"), a bull-free and practically tourist-free festival centered on the church of San Fermín de Aldapa (located behind the Mercado Santo Domingo on Calle Aldapa). Used only for Mass the rest of the year (and housing little of interest except a small statue of the saint), this church opens its doors each fall to become the heart of a celebration involving concerts, brass-band and food competitions, and parades of giant mannequins.

Laundry: Txukun is conveniently located on the main square (soap included, daily 8:00-22:00, last wash at 21:00, Plaza del Castillo 10, mobile +34 688 887 000).

Local Guide: Francisco Glaría is a top-notch guide and simply a delight to be with (€140/half-day up to 4 hours, extra for San Fermín and holidays, mobile +34 629 661 604, www.novotur. com).

Pamplona Walk

Even if you're not in town for the famous San Fermín festival, you can still get a good flavor of the town by following in the foot- and hoof-steps of its participants. This self-guided walk takes you through the town center along the same route of the famous Running of the Bulls.

• *Begin by the river, at the...*

Bull Corral: During the San Fermín festival, the bulls are released from here at 8:00 each morning (the rest of the year, it's a parked-car corral). They first run up Cuesta de Santo Domingo; signs labeled *El Encierro* mark their route. Follow them.

• *A few blocks ahead on the right is the...*

Museum of Navarre (Museo de Navarra): This museum, worth ▲, has four floors of artifacts and paintings celebrating the art of Navarre, from prehistoric to modern (€2, free Sat afternoons and all day Sun, open Tue-Sat 9:30-14:00 & 17:00-19:00, Sun 11:00-14:00, closed Mon, Santo Domingo 47, +34 848 426 492, www.museodenavarra.navarra.es). Formerly a 16th-century hospital, the building retains its original Renaissance entrance. Art is displayed chronologically: prehistoric tools and pottery and Roman mosaics on the first floor, Gothic and Renaissance artifacts along with castle frescoes on the second floor, Baroque and 19th- and 20th-century works (including Goya's painting *Retrato de Marqués de San Adrián*) on the third floor, and 20th- and 21st-century paintings by local artists on the top floor. The ground floor hosts free rotating exhibitions, often of modern art. Spacious and well arranged, the museum can be toured within an hour—consider circling back here after our walk.

Check out the **adjoining church** (on the left as you exit, show museum ticket), with its impressive golden Baroque-Rococo altar-piece depicting the Annunciation.

• *Continue along Cuesta de Santo Domingo. Embedded in the wall on your right, look for the small shrine containing an image of San Fermín. Farther up on your left is the **food market of Santo Domingo**, a handy spot to buy picnic supplies, including fine local cheeses (supermarket upstairs, market stalls downstairs). Ahead in the square is...*

City Hall (Ayuntamiento): When Pamplona was just starting out, many Camino pilgrims who had been "just passing through" decided to stick around. They helped build the city you're enjoying today but tended to cling to their own regional groups, which squabbled periodically. So in 1423, the king of Navarre (Charles III) tore down the internal walls and built a City Hall here to unite the community. This version (late Baroque, from the 18th century) is highly symbolic: Hercules demonstrates the city's strength, while the horn blower trumpets Pamplona's greatness.

The festival of San Fermín begins and ends on the balcony of this building (with the flags). Next to the TI are some of the barricades used during festivi-

ties. Look in the direction you just came from (the route of the bulls), and find the line of metal squares in the pavement—used to secure barricades for the run. There are four rows on this square, creating two barriers on each side. The inner space is for journalists and emergency medical care; spectators line up along the outer barrier. This first stretch is uphill, allowing the bulls to use their strong hind legs to pick up speed.

• *Follow the route of the bulls two blocks down Calle de Mercaderes to the intersection with Calle de la Estafeta. (Note that if you want to side-trip to the cathedral—described later, under "Sights in Pamplona"—it's dead ahead, three blocks up the skinny lane called "Curia" from this corner.) Turn right onto...*

Calle de la Estafeta: At this turn, the bulls—who are now going downhill—begin to lose their balance, often sliding into the barricade. Once the bulls regain their footing, they charge up the middle of La Estafeta. Notice how narrow the street is: No room for barricades...no escape for the daredevils trying to outrun the bulls.

On days that the bulls aren't running, La Estafeta is one of the most appealing streets in Pamplona. It's home to some of the best tapas bars in town (see "Eating in Pamplona," later). Because the old town was walled right up until 1923, space in here was at a premium—making houses tall and streets narrow.

Partway down the first block on the right, look for the hole-in-the-wall **Pastas Caseras Beatriz** shop (at #22)—most locals just call it "Beatriz"—makers of the best treats in Pamplona. Anything with chocolate is good, but the mini croissants are sensational. They come in three types: *garrotes de chocolate*, filled with milk chocolate; *cabello de angel*, filled with sweet pumpkin fibers; and *manzana*, apple. So simple...but oh so good.

Halfway down the street, notice the alley on the right leading to the main square (we'll circle back to the square later).

• *La Estafeta eventually leads you right to Pamplona's...*

Bullring (Plaza de Toros): Here's where the bulls meet their fate, but it's used for bullfights only nine days each summer (during the festival). The original arena from 1923 was expanded in the

The Symbols of Santiago

The pilgrim route leading to Santiago de Compostela—and the city itself—are rife with symbolism. Here are a few of the key items you'll see along the way.

St. James: The Camino's namesake is also its single biggest symbol. St. James can be depicted three ways: as a pilgrim, as an apostle, and as a Crusader (slaughtering Moors).

Scallop Shell (Vieira): The scallop shell is the symbol of St. James. Figuratively, the various routes from Europe to Santiago come together like the lines of a scallop shell. And literally, scallops are abundant on the Galician coast. Though medieval pilgrims carried shells with them only on the return home—to prove they'd been here and to scoop water from wells—today's pilgrims also carry them on the way to Santiago. The yellow sideways shell that looks like a starburst marks the route for bikers.

Gourd: Gourds were used by pilgrims to drink water and wine.

Yellow Arrow: These arrows direct pilgrims at every intersection from France to Santiago.

Red Cross: This long, skinny cross with curly ends at the top and sides, and ending in a sword blade at the bottom, represents the Knights of Santiago. This 12th-century Christian military order had a dual mission: to battle Muslim invaders while providing hospice and protection to pilgrims along the Camino de Santiago.

Tomb and Star: St. James' tomb (usually depicted as a simple coffin or box), and the stars that led to its discovery, appear throughout the city of Santiago, either together or separately.

1960s (see the extension at the top), doubling its capacity and halving its architectural charm.

Look for the big bust of **Ernest Hemingway,** celebrated by Pamplona as if he were a native son. Hemingway came here for the first time during the 1923 Running of the Bulls. Inspired by the spectacle and the gore, he later wrote about the event in his classic *The Sun Also Rises.* He said that he enjoyed seeing two wild animals running together: one on two legs, and the other on four. This literary giant put Pamplona and its humble, obscure bullfighting festival on the world map; visitors come from far and wide even today, searching for adventure in Hemingway's Pamplona. He came to his last Running of the Bulls in 1959 and reportedly regretted the attention his writing had brought to what had been a simple local festival. But the people of Pamplona appreciate "Papa" as one of their own. At the beginning of the annual festival, young people tie a red neckerchief around this statue so Hemingway can be properly outfitted for the occasion.

If you've always wanted to **tour a bullring,** this is your chance. The city recently opened an exhibit (worth ▲) that gives a behind-the-scenes look at this iconic space. At the start, you'll go down the same ramp and through the same red door that the bulls do during the festival. Once inside, you'll view a video showing historic and modern footage from the running of the bulls. Then you'll enter the corral where the bulls are held prior to the bullfight. In the stable, another video portrays the life of a bull from its simple *Ferdinand* existence in the countryside to its sudden end. The displays also explain the different stages of a bullfight and its major players. Just before you enter the arena, walk by the chapel where the toreadors say their prayers before entering the ring. Once you're out on the sand, go to the center and yell "Olé!" to test the great acoustics. Look for section number 2, where Hemingway used to sit so he could hear the workers comment on the strengths and weaknesses of the different bulls (€6, audioguide included, April-Oct Tue-Sat 10:30-19:30, Sun until 14:30, closed Mon; Feb-March weekends only 10:30-14:30, closed Nov-Jan; the bullring may close for special events, +34 948 225 389, www.feriadeltoro.com).

During the festival, **bullfights** start at 18:30, and tickets are expensive. But the price plummets if you buy tickets from scalpers after the first or second bull. The audience at most bullfights is silent, but Pamplona's spectators are notorious for their raucous behavior. They're known to intentionally spill things on tourists just to get a reaction...respond with a laugh and a positive attitude, and you'll earn their respect—and you'll probably have the time of your life.

• *For a peek at some of the old city fortifications that define Pamplona, take a detour behind the bullring to see the Fort of San Bartolomé (described on page 73). Otherwise, walk 20 yards while keeping the bullring on your left, then cross the busy street and walk a block into the pedestrian zone (on Avenida de Roncesvalles) to the life-size...*

Running of the Bulls Monument (Monumento al Encierro): This statue (pictured on page 70) shows 6 bulls, 2 steers, and 10 runners in action. Find the self-portrait of the sculptor (bald, lying down, and about to be gored). The statue has quickly become a local favorite but is not without controversy: There are 10 *mozos* but no *mozas*—where are the female runners?

• *Facing the monument, you can turn right and walk two blocks up the street to the main square...*

Plaza del Castillo: While not as grand as Spain's top squares,

Pamplona's has something particularly cozy and livable about it. It's dominated by the Navarre government building (sort of like a state capitol). Several Hemingway sights surround this square. The recommended Gran Hotel La Perla, in the corner, was his favorite place to stay. It recently underwent a head-to-toe five-star renovation, but Hemingway's room was kept exactly as he liked it, right down to the furniture he used while writing...and two balconies overlooking the bull action on La Estafeta street. He also was known to frequent Bar Txoko at the corner opposite La Perla (as well as pretty much every other bar in town) and the venerable Café Iruña. The recommended Café Iruña actually has a separate "Hemingway Corner" room, with a life-size statue of "Papa" to pose with.

• *You've survived the run. Now enjoy the rest of Pamplona's sights.*

Sights in Pamplona

▲Pamplona Cathedral (Catedral de Pamplona)

The Camino de Santiago is lined with great cathedrals, making Pamplona's feel like an architectural also-ran. However, after an expensive makeover, it looks like new and holds an interesting museum with a thoughtful message for pilgrims and tourists alike.

Cost and Hours: Cathedral and museum-€5, daily 10:30-19:00, until 17:00 in winter, museum closed Sun and during church services, last entry one hour before closing, let ticket office know if you want to do the 11:15 bell tower climb (you will need to take a number), +34 948 212 594, www.catedraldepamplona.com.

Visiting the Cathedral: The cathedral—a Gothic core wrapped in a Neoclassical shell—is shiny and clean from the outside, but the interior is dark and mysterious. Follow signs for *entrada* at the left side of the main entrance, buy your ticket, and go inside.

The prominent **tomb** dominating the middle of the nave holds Charles III (the king of Navarre who united the disparate groups of Pamplona) and his wife. The blue fleur-de-lis pattern is a reminder that the kings of Navarre once controlled a large swath of France. Notice that Charles' face is realistic, indicating that it was sculpted while he was still alive, whereas his wife's face is idealized—done after she died. Around the base of the tomb, monks from various orders mourn the couple's death.

In the **choir,** look for the silver and gold statue nicknamed

The Running of the Bulls: Fiesta de San Fermín

"A San Fermín pedimos, por ser nuestro patrón, nos guíe en el encierro, dándonos su bendición."
"We ask San Fermín, because he is our Patron, to guide us through the Running of the Bulls, giving us his blessing."

-Song sung before the run

For nine days each July, a million visitors pack into Pamplona to watch a gang of reckless, sangria-fueled adventurers thrust themselves into the path of an oncoming herd of furious bulls. Locals call it El Encierro (literally, "the enclosing"—as in, taking the beasts to be enclosed in the bullring)...but everyone else knows it as the "Running of the Bulls."

The festival begins at City Hall at noon on July 6, with various events filling the next nine days and nights. Originally celebrated as the feast of San Fermín—who is still honored by a religious procession through town on July 7—it has since evolved into a full slate of live music, fireworks, general revelry, and an excuse for debauchery. After dark the town erupts into a rollicking party scene. To beat the heat, participants chug refreshing sangria or kalimotxo (*calimocho* in Spanish)—half red wine, half cola. The town can't accommodate the crowds, so some visitors day-trip in from elsewhere (such as San Sebastián), and many young tourists simply pass out in city parks overnight (public showers are on Calle Hilarión Eslava in the old town).

The Running of the Bulls takes place each morning of the festival and is broadcast nationwide on live TV. The bulls' photos appear in the local paper be-  forehand, allowing runners to size up their opponents. If you're here to watch, stake your claim at a vantage point along the outer barrier by 6:30 or 7:00 in the morning. Don't try to stand along the inner barrier—reserved for press and medical personnel—or you'll be evicted when the action begins.

Before the run starts, runners sing a song to San Fermín (see lyrics above) three times to ask for divine guidance. Soon the bulls will be released from their pen near Cuesta de Santo Domingo. From here they'll stampede a half-mile through the town center...with thrill-seekers called *mozos* (and female *mozas*) running in front of the herd, trying to avoid a hoof or horn in the rear end.

Mozos traditionally wear white with strips of red tied around their necks and waists, and carry a newspaper to cover the bull's eyes when they're ready to jump out of the way. Two legends explain the red-and-white uniform: One says it's to honor San Fermín, a saint (white) who was martyred (red); the other says that the runners dress like butchers, who began this tradition. (The bulls are color-blind, so they don't care.)

At 8:00, six bulls are set loose. The beginning of the run is marked by two firecrackers—one for the first bull to leave the pen, and another for the last bull. The animals charge down the street, while the *mozos* try to run in front of them for as long as possible before diving out of the way. The bulls are kept on course by fencing off side-streets (with openings just big enough for mozos to escape). Shop windows and doors are boarded up.

A bull becomes most dangerous when separated from the herd. For this reason, a few steers—who are calmer, slower, have bigger horns, and wear a bell—are released with the bulls, and a few more trot behind them to absorb angry stragglers and clear the streets. (There's no greater embarrassment in this *muy* macho culture than to think you've run with a bull...only to realize later that you actually ran with a steer.)

The bulls' destination: the bullring...where they'll be ceremonially slaughtered as the day's entertainment.

If you're considering running with the bulls, it's essential to equip yourself with specific safety information not contained in this book. Locals suggest a few guidelines: First, understand that these are very dangerous animals, and running with them is entirely at your own risk. Be as sober as possible, and wear good shoes to protect your feet from broken glass and from being stepped on by bulls and people. (Runners wearing sandals might be ejected by police.) You're not allowed to carry a backpack, as its motion could distract the bulls. If you fall, wait for the animals to pass before standing up—it's better to be trampled by six bulls than to be gored by one. Ideally, try to get an experienced *mozo* to guide you on your first run.

Cruel as this all seems to the bulls—who scramble for footing on the uneven cobblestones as they rush toward their doom in the bullring—the human participants don't come away unscathed, either. Each year, dozens of people are gored, trampled, or otherwise injured. Over the last century, 15 runners have been killed at the event. But far more people have died from overconsumption of alcohol.

The festival ends at midnight on July 14, when the townspeople congregate in front of the City Hall, light candles, and sing their sad song, "Pobre de Mí": "Poor me, the Fiesta de San Fermín has ended."

"Mary of the Adopted Child." The Baby Jesus was stolen from this statue in the 16th century and replaced with a different version... which looks nothing like his mother. (The mother, dating from the 13th century, is the only treasure surviving from the previous church that stood on this spot.)

In the back-left corner chapel, dedicated to San Juan Bautista, find the Renaissance **crucifix**—shockingly realistic for a no-name artist of the time (compare it with the more typical one in the next chapel). The accuracy of Christ's musculature leads some to speculate that the artist had a model. (When you drive a nail through a foot, toes splay as you see here...but this is rarely seen on other crucifixes of the time.) It's said that if the dangling lock of hair touches Jesus' chest, the world will end.

Leave the cathedral and head to the **museum,** in the former cloister and attached buildings. The exhibits document the origins of Western thought and religion without focusing on one particular civilization or geographic area. Pass the spiral staircase into a room that chronicles the stages of cathedral construction. Next, wander through the Gothic cloister to the Archaeology Hall and the main exhibit.

Ramparts View: Exit to the left of the cathedral, walking through the tree-lined square and down picturesque Calle del Redín. Continue to the small viewpoint overlooking the Caballo Blanco ramparts. This is your best chance to see part of Pamplona's imposing **city walls**—designed to defend against potential invaders from the Pyrenees, still 80 percent intact, and now an inviting parkland. Belly up to the overlook, with views across the city's suburban sprawl. Beyond those hills on the horizon to the left are San Sebastián and the Bay of Biscay. Camino pilgrims enter town through the Puerta de Francia gate below and on the left. This area is popular with people who are in town for the Running of the Bulls but didn't make hotel reservations. Sadly, it was not unusual for people to fall asleep on top of the wall...then roll off to their deaths. The hodgepodge fencing here is designed to prevent that from happening during the next festival.

Church of San Saturnino

As a prominent town on the Camino route, Pamplona has its share of other interesting pilgrim churches. This one, the most important of the bunch, is an architectural combination: a 15th-century Gothic body with an 18th-century Baroque altar. Duck inside: This is where pilgrims can get their credential stamped (someone's usually on duty in the pews). At the end across from where you enter, you'll see an altar with the silver-bodied, golden-haloed Holy Virgin of the Camino. As you continue your journey, you'll notice that most churches along the Camino are dedicated to Mary. According to legend, when St. James himself came on a missionary trip through northern Spain, he suffered a crisis of faith around Zaragoza (not far from here). But, inspired by the Virgin, he managed to complete his journey to Galicia. Pilgrims following in his footsteps find similar inspiration from Mary today.

Cost and Hours: Free, Mon-Sat 9:15-12:00 & 18:00-19:30, Sun 10:00-13:30 & 18:30-19:30, Calle San Saturnino 3 (just off City Hall Square), +34 948 221 194, http://iglesiasansaturnino. com.

Church of San Lorenzo

San Fermín is a big name in town, and you'll find him in a giant side chapel of this church. Enter the church and turn right down the transept to find the statue of San Fermín, dressed in red and

wearing a gold miter (tall hat). Pamplona was founded by the Roman emperor Pompey (hence the name) in the first century BC. Later, a Roman general here became the first in the empire to allow Christians to worship openly. The general's son—Fermín—even preached the word himself... until he was martyred. Fermín has been the patron saint here ever since. Just below the statue's Adam's apple, squint to see a reliquary holding Fermín's actual finger. The statue—gussied up in an even more over-the-top miter and staff—is paraded around on Fermín's feast day, July 7, which was the origin of today's bull festival. This chapel is the most popular place in town for weddings.

Cost and Hours: Free, daily 8:15-12:30 & 17:30-20:30, overlooking the ring road at the edge of the old town at Calle Mayor 74, +34 629 443 777, www.capillasanfermin.com.

Fort of San Bartolomé (Fortín de San Bartolomé)

Pamplona is still defined by its remarkably preserved fortifications, considered some of the finest in Europe. A stroll through the city center often brings walls and gates into view. A large citadel protects the hard-to-defend southwest corner of the old town and has become one of the city's most enjoyed green spaces. The city walls, originally dividing three separate towns, were combined under the reign of Charles III. Centuries later, a constant threat from nearby France forced the city to adopt French defensive measures: a star-shaped wall inspired by France's Vauban fortifications.

Cost and Hours: Interior likely closed for renovation—check with TI for the latest, Calle Arrieta, www.pamplona.es.

Sleeping in Pamplona

Because Pamplona is a business-oriented town, prices go up during the week; on weekends, you can usually score a discount. All prices go way, way up for the San Fermín festival, when you must book as far in advance as possible.

$$$$ Gran Hotel La Perla is the town's undisputed top splurge. Hemingway's favorite hotel, sitting right on the main square, offers 44 posh rooms at Pamplona's best address (air-con, elevator, restaurant, Plaza del Castillo 1, +34 948 223 000, www.granhotellaperla.com, informacion@granhotellaperla.com). Well-heeled lit lovers can drop a bundle for a night in the Hemingway room, still furnished as it was when "Papa" stayed there (with a brand-new bathroom grafted on the front).

$$$ At **Palacio Guendulain,** pander to your inner aristocrat; this hotel is owned by the Count of Guendulain. Currently living in Madrid, he had his mansion in Pamplona converted into a luxurious 25-room hotel decorated with family crests, antiques, Spanish Old Masters, and ultramodern bathrooms. Check out the collection of carriages in the courtyard (air-con, elevator, restaurant open to nonguests, Zapatería 53, +34 948 225 522, www.palacioguendulain.com).

$$ Hotel Pompaelo Urban Spa has 30 modern rooms located just next to the City Hall. The hotel has a sky-bar with *vistas buenas,* and a free spa for hotel guests in the basement. The reception area and some of the rooms include historical walls from the old city tower (air-con, elevator, Plaza Consistorial 3, +34 848 473 137, www.hotelpompaelo.com, reservas@hotelpompaelo.com).

$ Hostal Navarra is the best value in Pamplona, with 14 modern, well-maintained, clean rooms. Near the bus station, but an easy walk from the old town, it's well run by well-spoken Miguel (RS%, check-in from 14:00, reception closes at 22:00—notify if you'll be arriving later, Calle Tudela 9, mobile +34 627 374 878, www.hostalnavarra.com, info@hostalnavarra.com).

$ Hotel Europa, a few blocks off the square, offers 25 rooms with reasonable prices for its green-marble elegance and ideal location (air-con, elevator, Calle Espoz y Mina 11, +34 948 221 800, www.hoteleuropapamplona.com, europa@hreuropa.com). The ground-floor restaurant is a well-regarded splurge among locals.

$ Hotel Yoldi is a comfortable business-style hotel in a 19th-century building. Well located just off Plaza Príncipe de Viana, its 50 modern rooms are handy for travelers arriving by bus from the train station (elevator, café, Avenida de San Ignacio 11, +34 948 224 800, www.hotelyoldi.com, yoldi@hotelyoldi.com).

$ Hotel Castillo de Javier, right on the bustling San Nicolás bar street (request a quieter back room), rents 19 small, simple yet lovely rooms (air-con, elevator, Calle San Nicolás 50, +34 948 203 040, www.hotelcastillodejavier.com, info@hotelcastillodejavier.com). This is a step up from the several cheap *hostales* that line the same street.

Eating in Pamplona

Typical specialties in Pamplona are *piquillo* (red peppers), white asparagus, and *menestra* (vegetable stew). Try the Navarran *Roncal* cheese and finish off your meal with a local dessert: *pantxineta* (a custard and almond tart) or *txantxigorri* (a cake made of lard, bread dough, and sugar). Try these with a fine Navarran wine or the local, sloe-flavored *pacharán* liqueur—considered a good digestif.

All the eateries listed here are within a couple minutes' walk of one another, and the tapas bars make a wonderful little pub crawl.

TAPAS CRAWL

On Calle de la Estafeta: The best concentration of trendy tapas bars is on and near the skinny drag called La Estafeta. My favorites here are **$$ Bar Cervecería La Estafeta** (try the *gulas*—baby eels—stuffed in a red pepper, daily, at #54, +34 948 222 157) and **$$ Bodegón Sarría,** where you'll lick your lips for *escombro,* a hot sandwich with Iberian ham and chorizo (English menu, dining room to enjoy Navarran dishes, at #50, +34 948 227 713).

Near Plaza del Castillo: A proud little prizewinning place, **$$ Bar Gaucho** serves gourmet tapas cooked to order. You could sit down, enjoy three tapas, and have an excellent meal. I never pass up the *huevo con trufo*—stir the truffle into the egg to get the full effect of the flavors (daily, just a few steps off the main square at Calle Espoz y Mina 7, +34 948 225 073).

$$ Café Roch is a time-warp eatery with a line of delightful tapas. Their most popular are the stuffed pepper and the fried Roquefort (daily, find the tobacco shop at #35 on Plaza del Castillo—Café Roch is a block away on the left at Calle de las Comedias 6, +34 948 222 390).

The narrow and slightly seedy Calle San Nicolás has more than its share of hole-in-the-wall tapas joints, with an older, more traditional clientele and homier, more straightforward tapas. **$$ La Mandarra de la Ramos** ("Ramos' Apron"), at #9, is a pork lover's paradise, where cured legs dangle enticingly over your head. Ham it up with a couple of *tostadas de jamón*, best washed down with a glass of the local *vino tinto* (daily, just around the corner from Café Roch, +34 948 212 654).

$$ Catachu serves ample portions in a simple but eclectic setting (menus more expensive on weekends, open daily, Calle Lindachiquia 16, +34 948 226 028).

Near the Cathedral: Seafood lovers can go to **$$ La Mejillonera,** where they can enjoy a *caña* (small draft beer) and *media* (half-portion) *de calamares bravos* in its simple, homey atmosphere. The deep-fried mini calamari are the perfect vehicle for picking up all that mayo and hot sauce (daily, Mon dinner only, Calle Navarrería 12, +34 948 229 184).

$$ La Capilla transformed a former chapel into a pristine, white dining space. Step into the restaurant to peek at the grand chandelier, but stay at the bar for some of the most innovative tapas in the city. Go early to grab a seat facing the plaza (closed Sun for dinner and Mon-Tue all day, Calle Dos de Mayo 4, +34 948 987 404).

RESTAURANTS

$$$ Café Iruña, which clings to its venerable past and its connection to Hemingway (who loved the place), serves up drinks out on the main square and food in the delightful old 1888 interior. While the food is mediocre, the ambience is great. Find the little "Hemingway's Corner" (El Rincón de Hemingway) side eatery in back, where the bearded one is still hanging out at the bar (accessible only on weekends). Enjoy black-and-white photos of Ernesto, young and old, in Pamplona (open daily, Plaza del Castillo 44, +34 948 222 064, www.cafeiruna.com).

$$$ San Ignacio Restaurante is an excellent choice for a real restaurant, where Nuntxi serves local fare with an emphasis on seasonal products. Set in what was formerly a private home, this place is elegant and inviting (open daily for lunch 13:30-15:30, also for dinner Fri-Sat 21:00-23:00, reservations smart, facing the back of the Navarre government building at Avenida San Ignacio 4, +34 948 221 874, www.restaurantesanignacio.com).

$$$$ Restaurante Ábaco, run by top chef Jesús Íñigo, is a special splurge, having just received a Michelin star and one of the highest gastronomical prizes in Spain. It offers an inspiring menu of creative *pintxos* and larger dishes. A mixed interior of wood and steel gives the place a hip yet traditional feel that goes well with the food. Try the specialty *pintxo, esponja de anchoa*—an amazing anchovy sandwich (Tue-Sat 13:30-15:30 & 21:00-22:30, Sun 13:30-15:30, closed Mon, Calle Juan de Labrit 19, +34 948 855 825, www.abacorestaurante.com).

SWEETS

To satisfy a sugar craving, visit the **Pastas Caseras Beatriz** shop on Calle de la Estafeta, which sells delicious mini croissants *(garrotes)* with various sweet fillings (closed Sun, Calle de la Estafeta 22, +34 948 220 618; described earlier in my self-guided walk). Across the street is **Gurgur** (meaning the rumbling sound of a hungry belly), where you can find specialties such as *chorizo de Pamplona,* coffee caramels, *txantxigorri* cake, the local *pacharán* liqueur, and *Roncal* cheese—ask the owner Nacho to slice it up (daily until 21:00, Calle Estafeta 21, +34 948 207 992).

Layana summons passersby with the thick scent of sugar and butter. A line of locals often spills out the doors because they know that both the *pasta de nata* and the *pasta de mermelada* (cream-filled and marmalade-filled cookies) are worth the wait (closed Sun, Calle Calceteros 12, +34 948 221 124).

Churrero de Lerín serves the best *churros y chocolate* in Pamplona. The doughnut-like hoops are perfect with the thick, hot chocolate. Cleanse your palate with a free swig of sweet brandy from the *porrón,* a glass dispenser with a spout like a hummingbird's beak. Be sure to pour from high up and avoid touching your mouth to the spout. You're welcome to add graffiti to the walls...as long as you don't write about politics or religion (daily, Calle de la Estafeta 5, +34 618 434 976).

Pamplona Connections

Note that the bus station is closer to the old town than the train station, and that some connections are faster by bus.

From Pamplona by Bus to: St-Jean-Pied-de-Port (2/day, 1.5 hours, Alsa), **San Sebastián** (10/day, 1 hour, Alsa), **Bilbao** (6/day, 2 hours, La Burundesa), **Madrid** (10/day—most with transfer, 6 hours, Alsa), **Madrid Barajas Airport** (7/day, 5 hours, Alsa, buy online in advance—tickets sell out). Bus info: Alsa (www.alsa.es) and La Burundesa (www.laburundesa.com).

By Train to: Burgos (6/day, 2-3.5 hours—direct, faster trains in afternoon), **San Sebastián** (3/day, 2 hours), **Madrid** (6/day direct, 3.5 hours).

French Basque Country

Compared with the Spanish lands across the border, the French Basque Country (Le Pays Basque) seems French first and Basque second. You'll see less Euskara writing than in Spain, but these destinations have their own special spice, mingling Basque and French influences with beautiful rolling countryside and gorgeous beaches.

Just 45 minutes apart by car, San Sebastián and St-Jean-de-Luz bridge the Spanish and French Basque regions. Between them you'll find the functional towns of Irún (Spain) and Hendaye (France).

My favorite home base here is the central, comfy, and manageable resort village of St-Jean-de-Luz. It's a stone's throw to Bayonne (with its "bigger-city" bustle and good Basque museum) and the snazzy beach town of Biarritz. A drive inland rewards you with a panoply of adorable French Basque villages. And St-Jean-de-Luz is a relaxing place to "come home" to, with its mellow ambience, fine strolling atmosphere, and good restaurants.

St-Jean-de-Luz / Donibane Lohizune

St-Jean-de-Luz (san zhahn-duh-lewz) sits cradled between its small port and gentle bay. The days when whaling, cod fishing, and pirating made it wealthy are long gone, but don't expect a cute Basque backwater. Tourism has become the economic mainstay, and it shows. Pastry shops serve Basque specialties, and store windows proudly display berets (a Basque symbol). Ice-cream lickers stroll traffic-free streets, while soft, sandy beaches tempt travelers to toss their itineraries into the bay. The knobby little mountain La Rhune towers above the festive scene. Locals joke that if it's clear enough to see La Rhune's peak, it's going to rain, but if you can't see it, it's raining already.

The town has little of sightseeing importance, but it's a good base for exploring the Basque Country and a convenient beach and port town that provides the most enjoyable dose of Basque culture in France. The town fills with French tourists in July and August—especially the first two weeks of August, when it's practically impossible to find a room without a reservation made long in advance...or even to walk down the main street.

It Happened at Hendaye

If taking the train between the Spanish and French Basque regions, you'll change trains at the nondescript little Hendaye station. While it seems innocent enough, this was the site of a fateful meeting between two of Europe's most notorious 20th-century dictators.

In the days before World War II, Adolf Hitler and Francisco Franco maintained a diplomatic relationship. But after the fall of France, they decided to meet secretly in Hendaye to size each other up. On October 23, 1940, Hitler traveled through Nazi-occupied France, then waited impatiently on the platform for Franco's delayed train. The over-eager Franco hoped the Führer would invite him to join in a military alliance with Germany (and ultimately share in the expected war spoils).

According to reports of the meeting, Franco was greedy, boastful, and misguided, leading Hitler to dismiss him as a buffoon. Franco later spun the situation by claiming that he had cleverly avoided being pulled into World War II. In fact, his own incompetence is what saved Spain. Had Franco made a better impression on Hitler here at Hendaye, it's possible that Spain would have entered the war, which could have changed the course of Spanish, German, and European history.

Orientation to St-Jean-de-Luz

St-Jean-de-Luz's old city lies between the train tracks, the Nivelle River, and the Atlantic. The main traffic-free street, Rue Gambetta, channels walkers through the center, halfway between the train tracks and the ocean.

The only sight worth entering in St-Jean-de-Luz is the church where Louis XIV and Marie-Thérèse tied the royal knot. St-Jean-de-Luz is best appreciated along its pedestrian streets, lively squares, and golden, sandy beaches. With nice views and walking trails, the park at the far eastern end of the beachfront promenade at Pointe Ste. Barbe makes a good walking destination.

The small, untouristed town of Ciboure, across the river from St-Jean-de-Luz, holds little of interest (although fans of Maurice Ravel can hunt down his birthplace at Quai Maurice Ravel 27).

TOURIST INFORMATION

The helpful TI is next to the big market hall, along the busy Boulevard Victor Hugo (July-Aug Mon-Sat 9:00-12:30 & 14:00-18:00, Sun 10:00-13:00 & 15:00-18:00; shorter hours rest of the year, closed Sun Jan-March; 20 Boulevard Victor Hugo, +33 5 59 26 03 16, town info: www.saint-jean-de-luz.com, regional info: www.terreetcotebasques.com).

Dipping into France

If you're heading from Spain to France, you don't have to worry about currency changes—both use the euro—or lengthy border stops (although police might ask to see your passport on buses or trains going into Spain). Here are a few other practicalities:

Hours: France typically does not enjoy as substantial a "siesta" as Spain; shops may close for an afternoon break, but usually only for an hour. The French eat lunch and dinner closer to the European mainstream time (around 12:00-13:30 & 19:00-21:00)—much earlier than Spaniards do.

Hotel Tips: The French have a simple hotel-rating system based on amenities, indicated in this chapter by asterisks. One star is modest, two has most of the comforts, and three is generally a two-star place with a fancier lobby and more elaborately designed rooms. Four or five stars offer more luxury than you'll probably have time to appreciate.

Restaurant Tips: In France, if you ask for the *menu* (muh-new), you won't get a list of dishes; you'll get a fixed-price meal. *Menus,* which include three or four courses, are generally a good value if you're hungry: You'll get your choice of soup, appetizer, or salad; your choice of a few main-course options with vegetables; plus a cheese course and/or a choice of desserts. Service is included (*service compris* or *prix net*), but wine and other drinks generally are extra.

ARRIVAL IN ST-JEAN-DE-LUZ

By Train or Bus: From the train station, the pedestrian underpass leads to the bus station. From there, it's easy to get to the TI and the center of the old town (just a few blocks away).

By Car: Follow signs for *Centre-Ville*, then *Gare* and *Office de Tourisme*. The old town is not car-friendly, with one-way lanes that cut back and forth across pedestrian streets. It's best to park your car in the free parking lot next to the train tracks.

By Plane: The nearest airport is Biarritz-Anglet-Bayonne Airport, 10 miles to the northeast near Biarritz. The tiny airport is easy to navigate, with a useful TI desk (airport code: BIQ, www.biarritz.aeroport.fr). To reach St-Jean-de-Luz, you can take a public bus (€3, hourly on weekdays, half as many on weekends, 45 minutes, get off at the Halte Routière stop near the train station, www.transports-atcrb.com) or a 25-minute taxi ride (about €30).

HELPFUL HINTS

Market Days: The Les Halles covered market is open daily from 6:00 to 13:00 and offers everything from fresh fish and produce to regional specialty dried goods. On Tuesday and Friday

French Survival Phrases: Although some French Basques speak Euskara, most speak French in everyday life. You'll find these phrases useful:

English	French
Good day	*Bonjour* (bohn-zhoor)
Mrs. / Ma'am	*Madame* (mah-dahm)
Mr. / Sir	*Monsieur* (muhs-yuh)
Please	*S'il vous plaît* (see voo play)
Thank you	*Merci* (mehr-see)
I'm sorry	*Désolé* (day-zoh-lay)
Excuse me	*Pardon* (par-dohn)
Yes / No	*Oui / Non* (wee / nohn)
How much is it?	*Combien?* (kohn-bee-an)
Cheers!	*Santé!* (sahn-tay)
Goodbye	*Au revoir* (oh ruh-vwahr)
women / men	*dames/hommes* (dahm / ohm)
one / two / three	*un/deux/trois* (uhn / duh / trwah)
Do you speak	*Parlez-vous* (par-lay voo)
English?	*Anglais?* (ahn-glay)

mornings (and summer Saturdays) until about 13:00, there's also a street market. Farmers' stands spill through the streets from the market on Boulevard Victor Hugo, giving everyone a rustic whiff of "life is good."

Pharmacies: Several can be found on Rue Gambetta. Look for the green cross.

Laundry: Laverie Automatique du Port is at 4 Boulevard Thiers (self-service daily 7:00-21:00, change machine; full-service available Wed-Fri 9:30-12:00 & 14:30-18:00, Sat 9:30-12:00; mobile +33 6 80 06 48 36).

Car Rental: Avis, at the train station, is handiest (Mon-Sat 8:30-12:00 & 14:00-17:30, closed Sun, +33 5 59 26 79 66).

Tours in St-Jean-de-Luz

Tourist Train

A little tourist train does a 30-minute trip around town (€6, departs every 45 minutes from the port, runs April-Oct 10:30-19:00, no train Nov-March). It's only worth the money if you need to rest your feet.

FRENCH BASQUE COUNTRY

Bus Excursions

Le Basque Bondissant runs popular day-trip excursions, including a handy jaunt to the Guggenheim Bilbao (€38 round-trip, includes museum admission, Wed only, departs 9:00 from green bus terminal across the street from train station, returns 19:15). You can get information on other tours and buy tickets at the TI or online (+33 5 59 26 25 87, www.basque-bondissant.com). Advance reservations are recommended in winter, when trips are canceled if not enough people sign up.

Boat Trips

Le Passeur, at the port, offers unguided bay crossings to Socoa and Ciboure, with departures every 40 minutes (€2.50 each way, €20/10 trips—shareable among groups, runs mid-April-Sept; Quai Maréchal Leclerc, mobile +33 6 11 69 56 93). **Nivelle V** offers mini Atlantic cruises and excursions, including 3.5-hour fishing trips (€36) departing at 8:00. They offer two coastal excursions: a Basque Coast to Spain tour (€18, 2 hours, leaves at 14:00) and a Sea Cliff tour (€10, 45 minutes, leaves at 16:00). Get tickets at their portside kiosk (runs April-mid-Oct, reservations required July-Aug, Quai Maréchal Leclerc, mobile +33 6 09 73 61 81, www.croisiere-saintjeandeluz.com).

St-Jean-de-Luz Walk

To get a feel for the town, take this hour-long self-guided stroll. You'll start at the port and make your way to the historic church.

Port: Begin at the little working port (at Place des Corsaires, just beyond the parking lot). Pleasure craft are in the next port over, in Ciboure. Whereas fishing boats used to catch lots of whales and anchovies, now they take in sardines and tuna—and take tourists out on joyrides. Anchovies were once a big part of the fishing business, but were overfished nearly into extinction and have been protected by the EU for the last few years, leading to a gradual rebound.

St-Jean-de-Luz feels cute and nonthreatening now, but in the 17th century it was home to the Basque Corsairs. With the French government's blessing, these pirates who worked the sea—and enriched the town—moored here.

• *After you walk the length of the port, on your right is the tree-lined...*

Place Louis XIV: The town's main square, named for the king who was married here, is a hub of action that serves as the town's communal living room. During the summer, the bandstand features traditional Basque folk music and dancing at 21:00 (almost nightly July-Aug, otherwise Sun, schedule usually posted on bandstand). Facing the square is the City Hall (Herriko Etchea) and the

House of Louis XIV (he lived here for 40 festive days in 1660). A visit to this house is worthwhile only if you like period furniture, though it's only open for part of the year; the rest of the time the privately owned mansion is occupied by the same family that's had it for over three centuries (€6.50, generally June-Aug Wed-Mon 10:30-12:30 & 14:30-18:30, Sept-mid-Oct 11:00-15:00 & 16:00-17:00, closed Tue and mid-Oct-May, visits by 40-minute guided tour only, 4/day, in French with English handouts, +33 5 59 26 27 58, www.maison-louis-xiv.fr).

The king's visit is memorialized by a small black equestrian statue at the entrance of the City Hall (a miniature of the huge statue that marks the center of the Versailles courtyard). The plane trees, with truncated branches looking like fists, are cut back in the winter so that in the summer they'll come back with thick, shady foliage.

• *Opposite the port on the far side of the square is...*

Rue de la République: This historic lane leads from Place Louis XIV to the beach. Once the home of fishermen, today it's lined with mostly edible temptations. Facing the square, **Maison Adam** (at #4) still uses the family recipe to bake the chewy, almond-rich *macarons* Louis XIV enjoyed during his visit to wed Princess Marie-Thérèse in 1660. Get one for €1 or grab other sweets, such as the less historic but just as tasty *gâteau basque*—a baked tart with a cream or cherry filling. Their gourmet shop next door (at #6) has Basque delicacies, *tartelettes*, sandwiches, and wine—great for an epicurean picnic.

Don't eat your fill of dessert just yet, though, because farther down Rue de la République you'll find **Pierre Oteiza**, stacked with rustic Basque cheeses and meats from mountain villages (with a few samples generally out for the tasting, and handy €4 paper cones of salami or cheese slices—perfect for munching during this walk).

You'll likely eat on this lane tonight. The recommended **Le Kaiku,** the town's top restaurant, fills the oldest building in St-Jean-de-Luz (with its characteristic stone lookout tower), dating from the 1500s. This was the only building on the street to survive a vicious 1558 Spanish attack. Two cannons flank the upper end of the street, which may be from Basque pirate ships. Notice the photo of fisherwomen with baskets on their heads, who would literally run to Bayonne to sell their fresh fish.

• *Continue to the...*

Beach: A high embankment protects the town from storm waters, but generally the Grande Plage—which is lovingly groomed daily—is the peaceful haunt of sun-seekers, soccer players, and happy children. Walk along the elevated promenade (to the right). Various tableaux tell history in French. Storms (including a particularly disastrous one in 1749) routinely knocked down buildings.

FRENCH BASQUE COUNTRY

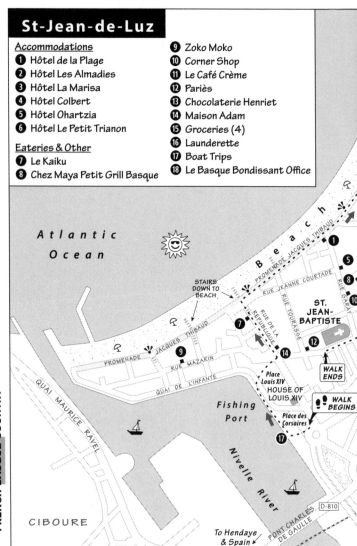

St-Jean-de-Luz

Accommodations
1. Hôtel de la Plage
2. Hôtel Les Almadies
3. Hôtel La Marisa
4. Hôtel Colbert
5. Hôtel Ohartzia
6. Hôtel Le Petit Trianon

Eateries & Other
7. Le Kaiku
8. Chez Maya Petit Grill Basque
9. Zoko Moko
10. Corner Shop
11. Le Café Crème
12. Pariès
13. Chocolaterie Henriet
14. Maison Adam
15. Groceries (4)
16. Launderette
17. Boat Trips
18. Le Basque Bondissant Office

Repeated flooding around 1800 drove the population down by two-thirds. Finally, in 1854, Napoleon III—who had visited here and appreciated the town—began building the three breakwaters you see today. Decades were spent piling 8,000 fifty-ton blocks, and by 1895 the town was protected. (But high tide and rough seas often break over the two bookend breakwaters, spraying water high into the sky.) To develop their tourist trade, they built a casino and a fine hotel, and even organized a special getaway train from Paris. During those days there were as many visitors as residents (3,000).

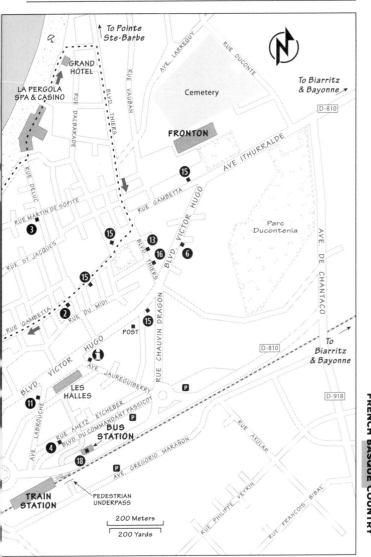

• Stroll through the seaside shopping mall fronting the late–Art-Deco-style La Pergola, which houses a casino, lots of shopping, expensive restaurants, the Hélianthal spa center (entrance around back), and overlooks the beach. Anyone in a white robe strolling the beach is from the spa. Beyond La Pergola is the pink, Neo-Romantic Grand Hôtel (c. 1900), with an inviting terrace for an expensive coffee break. From here circle back into town along Boulevard Thiers until you reach the bustling...

Rue Gambetta: Turn right down the pedestrianized street and circle back to your starting point, following the town's lively

Pelota

In keeping with the Basque people's seafaring, shipbuilding, and metalworking heritage, Basque sports are often feats of strength: Who can lift the heaviest stone? Who can row the fastest and farthest?

But the most important Basque sport of all is *pelota*—similar to what you might know as jai alai. Players in white pants and red scarves or shirts use a long, hook-shaped wicker basket (called a *txistera* in Euskara) to whip a ball (smaller and far bouncier than a baseball) back and forth off walls at more than 150 miles per hour. This men's-only game can be played with a wall at one or both ends of the court. Most matches are not professional, but betting on them is common. It can also be played without a racket—this handball version is used as a starter game for kids. Children use a bouncy rubber ball, while adults use a ball with a wooden center that's rather rough on the hands and needs a lot of strength to keep moving.

It seems that every small Basque town has two things: a church and a *pelota* court (called a *frontón*). While some *frontónes* are simple and in poor repair, others are freshly painted as a gleaming sign of local pride.

The TI in St-Jean-de-Luz sells tickets and has a schedule of matches throughout the area; you're more likely to find a match in summer (almost daily at 21:00 July-mid-Sept, afternoon matches sometimes on Sat-Sun). Matches are held throughout the year (except for winter) in the villages (ask for details at TI). The professional *cesta punta* matches on Tuesdays and Fridays often come with Basque folkloric halftime shows.

shopping strip. You'll notice many stores selling the renowned *linge Basque*—cotton linens such as tablecloths, napkins, and dishcloths, in the characteristic Basque red, white, and green. There are as many candy shops as there are tourists. Keep an eye open for a local branch of the British auction house Christie's, which specializes in high-end real estate. Video screens in the window advertise French castles for a mere €2 million, while local vacation homes go for considerably less.

• *Just before Place Louis XIV, you'll see the town's main church.*

Eglise St. Jean-Baptiste: The marriage of Louis XIV and Marie-Thérèse put St-Jean-de-Luz on the map, and this church is where it all took place. The ultimate in political marriages, the knot tied between Louis XIV and Marie-Thérèse in 1660 also cinched a reconciliation deal between Europe's two most powerful countries. The king of Spain, Philip IV—who lived in El Escorial palace—gave his daughter in marriage to the king of France, who lived in Versailles. This marriage united Europe's two largest palaces, which helped end a hundred years of hostility and forged an alliance that enabled both to focus attention on other matters (like England). Little St-Jean-de-Luz was selected for its 15 minutes of fame because it was roughly halfway between Madrid and Paris, and virtually on the France-Spain border. The wedding cleared out both Versailles and El Escorial palaces, as anyone who was anyone attended this glamorous event.

The church, centered on the pedestrian street Rue Gambetta, seems modest enough from the exterior...but step inside (free, Mon-Sat 8:00-12:00 &  14:00-18:30, Sun 8:00-12:00 & 15:00-19:00). The local expertise was in ship-building, so the ceiling resembles the hull of a ship turned upside-down. The dark wood balconies running along the nave segregated the men from the women and children (men went upstairs until the 1960s, as they still do in nearby villages) and were typical of Basque churches. The number of levels depended on the importance of the church, and this church, with three levels, is the largest Basque church in France.

The three-foot-long paddle-wheel ship hanging in the center was a gift from Napoleon III's wife, Eugènie. It's a model of an ill-fated ship that had almost sunk just offshore when she was on it. The box seats across from the pulpit were reserved for leading citizens who were expected to be seen in church and set a good example. Today the mayor and city council members sit here on festival Sundays.

The 1670 Baroque altar feels Franco-Spanish and features 20 French saints, with the city's patron saint—St. John the Baptist—placed prominently in the center. Locals in this proud and rich town call it the finest altar in the Basque Country. To see it better, pay €1 to switch on the automatic light (box next to the scene of the Crucifixion in the nave, on the right). The place has great acoustics, and the 17th-century organ is still used for concerts (a handful of concerts a year, get schedule at TI).

Leaving the church, turn left to find the bricked-up doorway—the church's original entrance. According to a quaint but untrue legend, it was sealed after the royal marriage (shown on the wall to the right in a photo of a painting) to symbolize a permanent closing of the door on troubles between France and Spain.

Sleeping in St-Jean-de-Luz

Hotels are more expensive here and breakfast costs extra. Those wanting to eat and sleep for less will do slightly better just over the border, in San Sebastián.

$$$ Hôtel de la Plage*** has the best location, right on the ocean. Its 28 rooms—22 with ocean view—have pleasant, fresh decor. The contemporary seaview breakfast room doubles as a comfortable lounge (family rooms, air-con, elevator, pay parking, 33 Rue Garat, +33 5 59 51 03 44, www.hoteldelaplage.com, reservation@hoteldelaplage.com, run by friendly Pierre, Laurent, and Frederic).

$$ Hôtel Les Almadies,*** on the main pedestrian street, is a bright boutique hotel with seven flawless rooms, comfy public spaces with clever modern touches, a pleasant breakfast room and lounge, an inviting sun deck, and a caring owner (good fans, pay parking—reserve in advance, 58 Rue Gambetta, +33 5 59 85 34 48, www.hotel-les-almadies.com, hotel.lesalmadies@wanadoo.fr, Bruno and Denise).

$$ Hôtel La Marisa*** is located on a quiet street a few steps from the beach. Its 16 rooms are filled with hardwood furniture and have maritime touches and a lavish feel. Enjoy its charming patio and small library (elevator, pay parking, 16 Rue Martin de Sopite, +33 5 59 26 95 46, www.hotel-lamarisa.com, info@hotel-lamarisa.com).

$$ Hôtel Colbert*** has 34 modern, tastefully appointed rooms across the street from the train station (family rooms, air-con, elevator, pay parking or park for free at lot next to train station, 3 Boulevard du Commandant Passicot, +33 5 59 26 31 99, www.hotelcolbertsaintjeandeluz.com, contact@hotelcolbertsaintjeandeluz.com).

$$ Hôtel Ohartzia** ("Souvenir"), one block off the beach, is comfortable, clean, and peaceful, with the most charming facade I've seen. It comes with 15 updated and well-cared-for rooms, generous and homey public spaces, plus a delightful garden. Upper rooms with a balcony have town and mountain views. Several rooms are 21st-century modern with vivid colors, and two have small interior terraces (elevator, 28 Rue Garat, +33 5 59 26 00 06, www.hotel-ohartzia.com, hotel.ohartzia@wanadoo.fr). Their front desk is technically open only 8:00-21:00, but owners Madame and Monsieur Audibert (who speak little English) live in the building; their son Benoît speaks English well.

\$\$ Hôtel Le Petit Trianon,** on a major street a couple of blocks above the old town's charm, is simple, bright, and *très sympa* (very nice), with 25 tidy rooms and an accommodating staff (family rooms, air-con, limited pay parking, closed mid-Nov-mid-Feb, 56 Boulevard Victor Hugo, +33 5 59 26 11 90, www.hotel-lepetittrianon.com, contact@hotel-lepetittrianon.com). To get a room over the quieter courtyard, ask for *côté cour* (koh-tay koor). Bus #816 has a convenient stop a half-block away.

Eating in St-Jean-de-Luz

St-Jean-de-Luz restaurants are known for offering good-value, high-quality cuisine. You can find a wide variety of eateries in the old center. For forgettable food with unforgettable views, choose from several places overlooking the beach. Most places serve from 12:15 to 14:00, and from 19:15 on. Remember, in France, *menu* means a fixed-price, multicourse meal.

The traffic-free Rue de la République, which runs from Place Louis XIV to the ocean promenade, is lined with hardworking restaurants (one of which is recommended next). Places are empty at 19:30, but packed at 20:30. Making a reservation, especially on weekends or in summer, is wise. Or consider a fun night of bar-hopping for dinner in San Sebastián instead (an hour away in Spain).

\$\$\$\$ Le Kaiku is *the* gastronomic experience in St-Jean-de-Luz. They serve modern, creatively presented cuisine, and specialize in wild seafood (rather than farmed). This dressy place, which owns a Michelin star, is the most romantic in town, but manages not to be stuffy (weekday fixed-price meals, closed Tue-Wed except July-Aug, 17 Rue de la République, +33 5 59 26 13 20, www.kaiku.fr, Nicolas). For the best experience, talk with your server about what you like best and your price limits (about €70 will get you a three-course meal *à la carte* without wine).

\$\$\$ Chez Maya Petit Grill Basque serves hearty traditional Basque cuisine. Their *ttoro* was a highlight of my day. They have *menus*, but à la carte is more interesting. If you stick around in warm weather, you'll see the clever overhead fan system kick into action (closed for lunch Mon and Thu and all day Wed, 2 Rue St. Jacques, +33 5 59 26 80 76).

\$\$\$\$ Zoko Moko offers Mediterranean nouvelle cuisine, with artistic creations on big plates. Get an *amuse-bouche* (an appetizer chosen by the chef) and a *mignardise* (a fun bite-sized dessert) with each main plate ordered. The lunchtime *menu du marché* changes weekly, depending on what's fresh in the market (€45 *menu* served all day; daily except closed Mon in winter; 6 Rue Mazarin, +33 5 59 08 01 23, www.zoko-moko.com, owner Charles).

FRENCH BASQUE COUNTRY

Fast and Cheap: Peruse the takeaway crêpe stands on Rue Gambetta. For a more elaborate crêpe, sit-down salad, or cheese-and-meat platter, try **$ Corner Shop** (daily 10:00-20:00, 22 Rue Garat, +33 6 75 42 76 73).

Breakfast: For a French-style breakfast with locals, head to the market house and find **$ Le Café Crème,** across from the market's main entrance (reasonable coffee, croissant, and fresh orange juice deal; Mon-Sat from 7:00, Sun from 9:30, 15 Avenue Labrouche, +33 5 59 26 10 75).

Sweets: Pariès is a favorite for its traditional sweets. Locals like their fine chocolates, *tartes, macarons,* fudge *(kanougas),* and *touron* (like marzipan, but firmer), which comes in a multitude of flavors—brought by Jews who stopped here just over the border in 1492 after being expelled from Spain. Their delectable *gâteau basque* is worth a try (9 Rue Gambetta, +33 5 59 26 01 46).

Chocolaterie Henriet has been a regional favorite since 1946. Walk into this quaintly elegant confectionary world and take your pick. Chocolates are priced per gram. My favorite is the *Rochers de Biarritz*—chocolate-covered roasted almonds with just a hint of orange (daily 10:00-19:00, Sun until 13:00, 10 Boulevard Thiers—just off of Rue Gambetta, +33 5 59 22 08 42).

Supermarkets: There are two small groceries: **Leader Price** is at the east end of Rue Gambetta near Boulevard Thiers, and **Petit Casino** is at Victor Hugo #46, a block from the post office (both Mon-Sat 8:00-13:00 & 15:00-19:30, closed Sun). **Monop',** a mini grocery store at 74 Rue Gambetta, has more selection and longer hours (Mon-Sat 8:30-late, Sun until 13:00). The bigger **Carrefour City** is at the intersection of Rue Gambetta and Boulevard Victor Hugo, near the recommended Hôtel Le Petit Trianon (Mon-Sat 7:00-21:00, Sun until 13:00).

St-Jean-de-Luz Connections

The train station in St-Jean-de-Luz is called St-Jean-de-Luz-Ciboure. Buses leave from the green building across the street; use the pedestrian underpass to get there. Bus and rail service is reduced on Sundays and off-season.

From St-Jean-de-Luz by Train to: Biarritz (nearly hourly, 20 minutes), **Bayonne** (hourly, 40 minutes), **St-Jean-Pied-de-Port** (4/day, 2.5 hours with transfer in Bayonne), **Paris** (5/day direct via high-speed TGV, 4.5 hours; more with transfer in Bordeaux, 6 hours), **Bordeaux** (hourly direct, 2.5 hours), **Sarlat** (4/day, 5-6 hours, transfer in Bordeaux), **Carcassonne** (5/day, 5-7 hours, transfer in Bordeaux or Toulouse).

By Train to San Sebastián: First, take the 10-minute train to the French border town of Hendaye (about 10/day). Or get to

Hendaye by bus (about hourly, 35 minutes, described next); check the schedule to see which leaves first.

Leave the Hendaye SNCF train station to the right and look for the small building on the same side of the street, where you'll catch the commuter EuskoTren into San Sebastián (usually 2/hour, runs about 7:00-22:30, 35 minutes).

By Bus: Transports64 buses leave from the bus station directly across from the train station. All tickets are bought from the driver. Bus #816 (or the express #816ee) connects St-Jean-de-Luz to **Biarritz**'s train station and **Bayonne** almost hourly. It also goes the opposite direction to **Hendaye** about hourly. Be sure to check times and final destinations on the well-displayed timetable at the bus stop post (fewer departures on weekends). Another bus connects St-Jean-de-Luz to **Sare** (Mon-Fri 5/day, fewer Sat-Sun, 30 minutes, www.hegobus.fr). BlaBlaBus runs buses to **San Sebastián** (Mon-Sat 3-5/day, fewer Sun, www.blablabus.com). Buses stop on the street in front of the green kiosk next to the bus station and take about 50 minutes.

By Excursion: If you're without a car, consider using **Le Basque Bondissant**'s day-trip excursions to visit otherwise difficult-to-reach destinations, such as the Guggenheim Bilbao (see "Tours in St-Jean-de-Luz," earlier).

By Taxi to San Sebastián: This will cost you about €75 for up to four people, but it's convenient (+33 5 59 26 10 11 or mobile +33 6 25 76 97 69).

ROUTE TIPS FOR DRIVERS

A one-day side trip to both Bayonne and Biarritz is easy from St-Jean-de-Luz. These three towns form a sort of triangle (depending on traffic, each one is less than a 30-minute drive from the other). Hop on the autoroute to Bayonne, sightsee there, then take D-810 into Biarritz. Leaving Biarritz, continue along the coastal D-810. In Bidart, watch (on the right) for the town's proud *frontón* (*pelota* court) and stop for a photo of the quaint Town Hall. Consider peeling off to go into the village center of Guéthary, with another *frontón* and a massive Town Hall. If you're up for a walk on the beach, cross the little bridge in Guéthary, park by the train station, and hike down to the walkway along the surfing beach (lined with cafés and eateries). When you're ready to move on, you're a very short drive from St-Jean-de-Luz.

Bayonne / Baiona

To feel the urban pulse of French Basque Country, visit Bayonne— modestly but honestly nicknamed "your anchor in the Basque Country" by its tourist board. With frequent, fast train and bus connections with St-Jean-de-Luz, Bayonne makes an easy half-day side trip.

Come here to browse through Bayonne's atmospheric and well-worn-yet-lively old town, and to admire its impressive Museum of Basque Culture. Known for establishing Europe's first whaling industry and for inventing the bayonet, Bayonne is more famous today for its ham *(jambon de Bayonne)* and chocolate.

Get lost in Bayonne's old town. In pretty Grand Bayonne, tall, slender buildings, decorated in Basque fashion with green-and-red shutters, climb above cobbled streets. Be sure to stroll the streets around the cathedral and along the banks of the smaller Nive River, where you'll find the market (Les Halles).

Orientation to Bayonne

Bayonne's two rivers, the grand Adour and the petite Nive, divide the city into three parts: St-Esprit, with the train station, and the more interesting Grand Bayonne and Petit Bayonne, which together make up the old town.

TOURIST INFORMATION

The modern TI sits alongside a lengthy parking lot one block off the mighty Adour River, on the northeastern edge of Grand Bayonne. They have very little in English other than a map and a town brochure, but there's always someone on staff who speaks English (July-Aug Mon-Sat 9:00-19:00, Sun 10:00-13:00; shorter hours and closed Sun in off-season; Place des Basques, +33 5 59 46 09 00, www.bayonne-tourisme.com). They sometimes offer a two-hour tour in English on summer Saturdays (€6, leaves at 15:00).

ARRIVAL IN BAYONNE

By Train: The TI and Grand Bayonne are a 15-minute walk from the train station. Walk straight out of the station, cross the parking lot and traffic circle, and then cross the imposing bridge (Pont St. Esprit). Once past the big Adour River, continue across a smaller bridge (Pont Mayou), which spans the smaller Nive River. Stop on Pont Mayou to orient yourself: You just left Petit Bayonne (left side of Nive River); ahead of you is Grand Bayonne (spires of cathedral straight ahead, TI a few blocks to the right). The Museum of Basque Culture is in Petit Bayonne, facing the next bridge up the Nive River.

By Car or Bus: The handiest parking is also where buses (and the electric Tram'Bus connecting Bayonne and Biarritz) arrive in Bayonne: next to the TI at the modern parking lot on the edge of Grand Bayonne. To reach the town center from here, walk past the war memorial and through the break in the ramparts. Follow the walkway until you reach a fancy gate that leads through a tunnel. After the tunnel, turn right at the next street; the cathedral should immediately come into view. Continue behind the cathedral and walk down, down, down any of the atmospheric streets to find Les Halles (the market) and the Nive River.

To reach this parking lot, **drivers** take the *Bayonne Sud* exit from the autoroute, then follow green *Bayonne Centre* signs, then white *Centre-Ville* signs (with an *i* for tourist information). You'll see the lot on your right. Payment machines only accept coins for a maximum of two hours. In high season, when this lot can be full, use one of the lots just outside the center (follow signs to *Glain*—€1/day—or *Porte d'Espagne* as you arrive in town), then catch the little orange *navette* (shuttle bus) to get into the center (free, find route maps posted at stops in town, every 8 minutes, Mon-Sat 7:30-19:30, none on Sun).

HELPFUL HINTS

Loaner Bikes: Although Bayonne's sights are easily reached on foot (except the chocolate workshop), pedaling about by bike is simple and relaxing. The TI lends a limited number of orange bikes for free to adults during office hours (must leave passport or driver's license, €150 deposit, www.cyclocom.com).

Laundry: Laverie is under a colonnade directly across the street from the TI (self-service, daily 7:00-21:00, 8 Place des Basques, mobile +33 6 08 46 02 51).

Local Guide: Fun and energetic **Claire Lohiague** can take you on a walking tour of Bayonne (€65/person for 2-3 hours, half-day tours available), or to nearby cities or villages in the French Basque Country (hotel pickup in her minivan, mobile +33 6 85 35 96 30, argibiliak@gmail.com).

Sights in Bayonne

▲Museum of Basque Culture (Musée Basque)

This museum (in Petit Bayonne, facing the Nive River at Pont Marengo) explains French Basque culture from cradle to grave—in French, Euskara, and Spanish. Ask to borrow the pamphlets with museum descriptions in English. Artifacts and videos take you into traditional Basque villages and sit you in the front row of time-honored festivals, letting you envision this otherwise hard-to-experience culture.

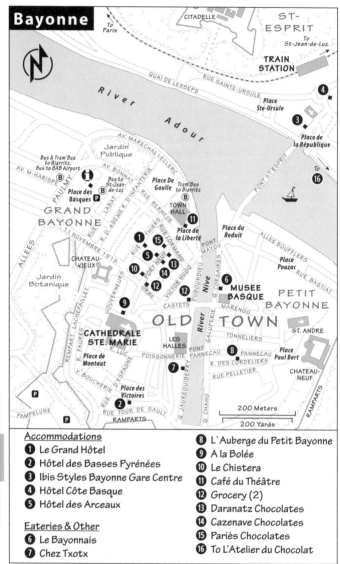

Accommodations
1 Le Grand Hôtel
2 Hôtel des Basses Pyrénées
3 Ibis Styles Bayonne Gare Centre
4 Hôtel Côte Basque
5 Hôtel des Arceaux

Eateries & Other
6 Le Bayonnais
7 Chez Txotx

8 L`Auberge du Petit Bayonne
9 A la Bolée
10 Le Chistera
11 Café du Théâtre
12 Grocery (2)
13 Daranatz Chocolates
14 Cazenave Chocolates
15 Pariès Chocolates
16 To L'Atelier du Chocolat

Cost and Hours: €7.50, free first Sun of month; open Tue-Sun 10:00-18:30, Oct-March until 18:00, closed Mon except July-Aug, last entry one hour before closing, 37 Quai des Corsaires, +33 5 59 59 08 98, www.musee-basque.com.

Visiting the Museum: On the ground floor, you'll begin with a display of carts and tools used in rural life, then continue past some 16th-century gravestones. Look for the *laiak*—distinctive forked hoes used to work the ground. At the end of this section you'll watch a grainy film on Basque rural lifestyles.

The next floor up begins by explaining that the house *(etxea)* is the building block of Basque society. More than just a building, it's a social institution—Basques are named for their houses, not vice versa. You'll see models and paintings of Basque houses, then domestic items, a giant door, kitchen equipment, and furniture (including a combination bench-table, next to the fireplace). After viewing an exhibit on Basque clothing, you'll move into the nautical life, with models, paintings, and actual boats. The little door leads to a large model of the port of Bayonne in 1805, back when it was a strategic walled city.

Upstairs you'll learn that the religious life of the Basques was strongly influenced by the Camino de Santiago pilgrim trail, which passes through their territory. One somber space explains Basque funeral traditions. The section on social life includes a video of Basque dances (typically accompanied by flute and drums). These are improvised, but according to a clearly outlined structure—not unlike a square dance.

The prominence given to the sport of *pelota* (see sidebar, earlier) indicates its importance to the Basque people. One dimly lit room shows off several types of *txistera* baskets (*chistera* in French), gloves, and balls used for the game; videos show you how these items are made. The museum wraps up with a brief lesson on the region's history from the 16th to the 20th century, including exhibits on the large Jewish population here (which had fled from a hostile Spain) and the renaissance of Basque culture in the 19th century.

Cathédrale Ste. Marie

Bankrolled by the whaling community, this cathedral sits dead-center in Grand Bayonne and is worth a peek. Centuries of construction and two major fires left nothing of the original Romanesque structure, and locals obtained stones from two different quarries (compare the colors in the facade). Find the unique keystones—reminders of British rule here in Aqui-  taine—on the ceiling along the nave, then circle behind the church to find the peaceful and polished 13th-century cloister. Restoration of this church will take several years, so expect some scaffolding and a few closed chapels.

Cost and Hours: Free, Mon-Sat 9:30-11:30 & 15:00-17:45,

Sun 16:00-17:45; cloister usually accessible one hour after church opens.

Sweets Shops

With no more whales to catch, Bayonne turned to producing mouthwatering chocolates and marzipan; look for shops on the arcaded Rue du Port Neuf (running between the cathedral and the Adour River). **Daranatz** is Bayonne's best chocolate shop, with bars of chocolate blended with all kinds of flavors—one with a general mix of spices (lots of cardamom), one with just cinnamon, and another with *piments d'Espelette* (15 Arceaux Port Neuf, +33 5 59 59 03 55). **Cazenave,** founded in 1854, is a fancy *chocolaterie* with a small café in the back. Try their foamy hot chocolate with fresh whipped cream on the side, served with buttered toast for €10. You can also share one order of toast and two chocolates (Tue-Sat 9:00-12:00 & 14:00-19:00, closed Sun-Mon, 19 Rue Port Neuf, +33 5 59 59 03 16). **Pariès,** well-known throughout France, got its start in Bayonne. Their bonbons rank among the best, but for something different try the cherry-jam-filled *gâteau basque* (Mon-Sat 9:00-19:00, Sun until 13:00, 14 Rue Port Neuf, +33 5 59 59 06 29).

Chocolate Workshop

L'Atelier du Chocolat is a chocolate factory and boutique in an industrial part of town. You'll see a detailed exhibit on the history and making of chocolate, some workers making luscious goodies (10:00-11:00 only), and a video in English on request. The generous chocolate tasting at the end is worth the ticket price for chocoholics.

Cost and Hours: €6, Mon-Sat 10:00-12:30 & 14:00-18:00, closed Sun, July-Aug no lunch break, last entry one hour before closing, 7 Allée de Gibéléou, +33 5 59 55 70 23, www.atelierduchocolat.fr. They also have a shop on Rue Port Neuf, along with the *chocolateries* mentioned above.

Getting There: Take city bus #A2 from the TI or the Mairie stop across from the Town Hall (buy €1.40 ticket on board), get off at the Jean Jaurès stop, walk under the railway bridge following the main road past the roundabout, and look for signs.

Ramparts

The ramparts around Grand Bayonne are open for walking and great for picnicking (access from park at far end of TI parking lot). However, the ramparts do not allow access to either of Bayonne's castles—both are closed to the public.

Sleeping in Bayonne

$$ Le Grand Hôtel**** is the best of the limited options in Bayonne—it's well located in Grand Bayonne, with all the comforts and a pleasant staff. While renovating their old building, the owners took care to maintain the original, classic decor (RS%—free breakfast for readers with this book, elevator, pay parking, 21 Rue Thiers, +33 5 59 59 62 00, www.legrandhotelbayonne.com, ha0y1@accor.com).

$$ Hôtel des Basses Pyrénées****** took an ageing, turn-of-the-century hotel and added plush, modern comforts. Their 26 rooms are suitably chic. Located on an open square, its adjoining restaurant also has a good reputation with locals (elevator, reserved pay parking, 12 Rue Tour de Salut, +33 5 59 25 70 88, www.hotel-bassespyrenees-bayonne.com, contact@hoteldesbassespyrenees.com).

$$ Ibis Styles Bayonne Gare Centre*** sits next to the Pont Saint Esprit, near the train station. Some of its 45 white, bright rooms overlook the river (includes breakfast, elevator, pay parking at train station lot, 1 Place de la République, +33 5 59 55 08 08, www.ibis.com, h8716@accor.com).

$ Hôtel Côte Basque** is conveniently located by the train station in the Saint Esprit neighborhood, just across the river from the old town. It's on a busy street, so its 40 small-but-comfortable rooms have double-paned windows to cut the noise (family rooms, elevator, pay parking, 2 Rue Maubec, +33 5 59 55 10 21, www.hotel-cotebasque.fr, contact@hotel-cotebasque.fr).

$ Hôtel des Arceaux,** run by friendly Frédéric, is a B&B-style establishment with 16 rooms on a small pedestrian street in Grand Bayonne. It's just across the street from recommended chocolate shops (26 Rue Port Neuf, +33 5 59 59 15 53, hotel.arceaux@wanadoo.fr).

Eating in Bayonne

The Grand Bayonne riverside has several tapas restaurants, a couple of easy *bistrots,* and a pizza place. The Petit Bayonne riverside has some *bistrots* and a few more proper sit-down restaurants. The pedestrian streets surrounding the cathedral in Grand Bayonne offer casual dining spots serving crêpes, *tartines,* quiches, and salads. Most places have outdoor tables in nice weather.

$$$ Le Bayonnais, next door to the Museum of Basque Culture, serves traditional Basque specialties à la carte. Sit in the blue-tiled interior or out along the river (weekday lunch specials and dinner *menu,* closed Sun-Mon, 38 Quai des Corsaires, +33 5 59 25 61 19).

$$ Chez Txotx (pronounced "choch") has a very Spanish-bodega ambience under a small chorus line of hams. You can also sit outside, along the river, just past the market hall (daily, 49 Quai Amiral Jauréguiberry, +33 5 59 59 16 80).

$$ L'Auberge du Petit Bayonne, tucked away on a little side street, is a local-style place with Basque "grandmother" recipes often consisting of cod, Bayonne ham, lamb, and trout. Eric takes care of the front of the house (and speaks some English), while his wife Cathy manages the kitchen (Thu-Sun 12:00-14:00 & 19:30-21:30, Fri-Sat until 22:00, closed Mon-Tue, 23 Rue des Cordelier, +33 5 59 59 83 44).

$$ A la Bolée serves up inexpensive sweet and savory crêpes in a cozy atmosphere along the side of the cathedral (daily, 10 Place Pasteur, +33 5 59 59 18 75).

$$$ Le Chistera, run by a family that's spent time in the US, proudly serves traditional Basque dishes made with market-fresh ingredients. Try the *poulet* with Basque sauce or one of their soups, and polish off your meal with homemade *gâteau basque* (good-value lunch *menu,* Tue-Sun 12:00-14:00, Thu-Sun also 19:30-21:00, closed Mon, 42 Rue Port Neuf, +33 5 59 59 25 93).

$$ Café du Théâtre has pleasant outdoor tables on a square by the river. Try it for a simple early breakfast or a delightful lunch with locals and office workers (daily 8:00-22:00, 8 Place de la Liberté, +33 5 59 59 60 00).

Picnic Supplies: If the weather's good, consider gathering a picnic from the shops along the pedestrian streets, at Les Halles market (daily, 7:00-13:30), in the Casino Shopping grocery store (daily 7:30-21:00, 2 Rue Port de Castets, also entrance on Rue Victor Hugo), or at the Monoprix (Mon-Sat 8:30-20:00, Sun 9:00-12:45, 8 Rue Orbe). Don't forget the chocolate, then head for the park around the ramparts below the *Jardin Botanique* (benches galore).

Bayonne Connections

Chronoplus buses run throughout the area regularly. Most lines run two to three times an hour from about 7:00 to 20:00 (less frequent Sat-Sun). Buy a €1.40 ticket on the bus; if you plan to ride twice or more in one day, buy the 24-hour ticket for €2.40 (www.chronoplus.eu).

From Bayonne by Bus to: BAB (Biarritz-Anglet-Bayonne) Airport (2-3/hour, 15 minutes, line #C is best option), **Biarritz** (5/hour, fewer on Sun, 30 minutes, Chronoplus lines #A1 and #A2; also possible by Tram'bus—see next), **St-Jean-de-Luz** (almost hourly, 45 minutes, Transports64 line #816 or express #816ee), and **San Sebastián** (4/day, fewer on Sun, 2.5 hours, 1 change, BlaBla-

Bus). Pick up BAB and Biarritz buses on the main avenue Allées Paulmy, behind the TI; catch the St-Jean-de-Luz and San Sebastián buses just in front of the TI. Buses to the inland Basque villages of Espelette and Ainhoa are impractical.

The electric **Tram'bus** is handy for day-trippers heading to **Biarritz**. Take line 1 (T1) from just behind the TI near Place des Basques or from the Mairie stop at the Town Hall (€1/one-hour pass, 3/hour, 30 minutes, runs daily 5:00-24:00, www.trambuspaysbasque.fr).

By Train to: St-Jean-Pied-de-Port (4/day, 1 hour).

By Taxi to: Biarritz (20 minutes, about €30), **St-Jean-de-Luz** (30 minutes, about €50—or more if traffic is heavy, +33 5 59 59 48 48).

Biarritz

A glitzy resort town steeped in the belle époque, Biarritz (bee-ah-ritz) is where the French Basques put on the ritz. In the 19th century, this simple whaling harbor became, almost overnight, a high-class aristocrat magnet dubbed the "beach of kings." Although St-Jean-de-Luz and Bayonne are more fully French and more fully Basque, the made-for-international-tourists,  jet-set scene of Biarritz is not without its charms. Perched over a popular surfing beach, anchored by grand hotels and casinos, hemmed in by jagged and picturesque rocky islets at either end, and watched over by a lighthouse on a distant promontory, Biarritz is a striking beach resort. However, for sightseers with limited time, it's likely more trouble than it's worth.

Orientation to Biarritz

Biarritz feels much bigger than its population of 30,000. The town sprawls, but virtually everything we're interested in lines up along the waterfront: the beach, the promenade, the hotel and shopping zone, and the TI.

Tourist Information: The TI is in a little pink castle two blocks up from the beach (July-Aug daily 9:00-19:00; shorter hours rest of the year; Square d'Ixelles, +33 5 59 22 37 10, www.tourisme. biarritz.fr). It's just above the beach and casino, hiding behind the City Hall—look for *hôtel de ville* signs.

FRENCH BASQUE COUNTRY

Arrival in Biarritz: If coming by **car,** follow signs for *Centre-Ville,* then carefully track signs for specific parking garages. The most central garages are called *Grande Plage, Casino, Bellevue,* and *St. Eugénie* (closest to the water). Signs in front of each tell you whether it's full *(complet);* if it is, move on to the next one.

Biarritz's **train** station is about two miles from town—you can connect to the city center (Mairie) on the Chronoplus bus #A1 (€1.40, buy ticket from driver, 3-4/hour). **Buses** from Bayonne (Chronoplus or the electric Tram'bus) stop at "Biarritz Mairie" near the TI; Transports64 #816 or #816ee buses from Hendaye and St-Jean-de-Luz stop near the train station (go downhill, take first left to find train station and Chronoplus bus stop described above). There is no baggage storage in Biarritz.

Sights in Biarritz

There's little of sightseeing value in Biarritz. The TI can fill you in on the town's four museums (Marine Museum—described below; Chocolate Planet and Museum—intriguing, but a long walk from the center; Oriental Art Museum—large, diverse collection of art from across Asia; and Biarritz Historical Museum—really?).

Your time is best spent strolling along the various levels that climb up from the sea. (Resist the urge to check out the pebble beach for now.) From the TI, you can do a loop: First head west on the lively **pedestrian streets** that occupy the plateau above the water, which are lined with restaurants, cafés, and high-class, resorty window-shopping. (Place Georges Clemenceau is the grassy "main square" of this area.) Biarritz is picnic-friendly, with *beaucoup* benches facing the waves. Consider stocking up before continuing this walk.

Work your way past the Église Sainte Eugénie out to the point with the **Marine Museum** (Musée de la Mer). The most conve-

nient of Biarritz's attractions, this pricey Art Deco museum/aquarium wins the "best rainy-day option" award, with a tank of seals and a chance to get face-to-teeth with live sharks (€15, generally daily 9:30-20:00, closes later in summer and earlier in winter, last entry one hour before closing, +33 5 59 22 75 40, www.aquariumbiarritz.com).

Whether or not you're visiting the museum, it's worth hiking down to the entrance, then wandering out on the walkways that connect the big offshore rocks. These lead to the so-called **Virgin of the Rock** (Rocher de la Vierge), topped by a statue of Mary.

From here stick along the water as you head back toward the TI. After a bit of up and down over the rocks, don't miss the trail down to **Fisherman's Wharf** (Port des Pêcheurs), a little pocket of salty authenticity that clings like barnacles to the cliff below the hotels. The remnants of an aborted construction project from the town's glory days, this little fishing settlement of humble houses and rugged jetties seems to faintly echo the Basque culture that thrived here before the glitz hit. Many of the houses have been taken over by the tourist trade (gift shops and restaurants).

Continuing along the water (and briefly back up to street level), make your way back to the town's centerpiece, the **big beach** (Grande Plage). Dominating this inviting stretch of sand is the Art Deco casino, and the TI is just above that. If you haven't yet taken the time to splash, wade, or stroll on the beach...now's your chance.

Eating in Biarritz

If you arrive early, head for **Les Halles,** a covered market great for picking up items for a picnic. Enjoy its bustling market vibe (daily 7:30-14:00, mid-July-Aug also open 18:00-21:00, 11 Rue des Halles). Many eateries surround the market, including **$$ Le Café du Commerce,** a good place for breakfast. A **Carrefour City** grocery store is also next to the market.

For lunch or a sit-down dinner, **$$$ La Table Basque** next to the TI is as Basque as it gets (Thu-Tue 12:00-13:45 & 19:15-21:30, closed Wed, 4 Avenue de la Marne, +33 5 59 22 23 52). For a meal by the sea, **$$ Casa Juan Pedro** serves up fresh seafood and meat dishes at the Fisherman's Wharf (generally daily 12:15-14:00 & 19:30-22:00, can get busy in high season, 48 Allée Port des Pêcheurs, +33 5 59 24 00 86).

Biarritz Connections

From Biarritz by Bus to: Bayonne (5/hour on Chronoplus lines #A1 and #A2, fewer on Sun, 30 minutes; about 3/hour on electric Tram'bus line 1, 30 minutes). See details under "Bayonne Connections," earlier.

By Train to: St-Jean-de-Luz (nearly hourly, 20 minutes; from the center, take Chronoplus bus #A1 to Biarritz train station, 3-4/hour; www.sncf.fr). It's also possible to reach St-Jean-de-Luz on Transports64 **bus** #816 or express #816ee (nearly hourly, fewer Sat-Sun, 35 minutes; bus stop is a 5-minute walk from the train station; www.transports64.fr).

Villages in the French Basque Country

Traditional villages among the green hills, with buildings colored like the Basque flag, offer the best glimpse of Basque culture. Cheese, hard cider, and *pelota* players are the primary products of these villages, which attract few foreigners but many French summer visitors. Most of these villages have welcomed pilgrims bound for Santiago de Compostela since the Middle Ages. Today's hikers trek between local villages or head into the Pyrenees. The most appealing villages lie in the foothills of the Pyrenees, spared from beach-scene development.

Use St-Jean-de-Luz as your base to visit the Basque sights described below. For information on another French Basque village a bit farther away—St-Jean-Pied-de-Port (Donibane Garazi), the starting point of the Camino de Santiago pilgrim trail—see page 104. You can reach some of these places by public transportation, but the hassle outweighs the rewards.

Do a circuit of these towns in the order they're listed here (and, with time, also add St-Jean-Pied-de-Port at the end). Assuming you're driving, I've included route instructions as well.

• *Only 15 minutes from St-Jean-de-Luz, follow signs for* Ascain, *then* Sare. *On the twisty-turny road toward Sare, you'll pass the station for the train up to...*

La Rhune/Larrun

Between the villages of Ascain and Sare, near the border with Spain, a small cogwheel train takes tourists to the top of La Rhune, the region's highest peak (2,969 feet). You'll putt-putt up the hillside for 35 minutes in a wooden, open-air train car to reach panoramic views of land and sea (€19.50 round-trip, runs daily March-mid-Nov only, departures weather-dependent—the trip is worthless if it's not clear, goes every 35 minutes when busiest July-Aug, +33 5 59 54 20 26, www.rhune.com). For those traveling without a car, buses run from St-Jean-de-Luz (take #21 from the bus station and get off at Col de Saint-Ignace; 7/day Mon-Sat, 4/day Sun, 20 minutes, www.hegobus.fr).

• *Continue along the same road and look for pull-offs with room for a couple of cars, typically placed at the most scenic spots. Stop to smell the grass before the next stop...*

Sare/Sara

Sare, which sits at the base of the towering mountain La Rhune, is among the most picturesque villages—and the most touristed. It's easily reached from St-Jean-de-Luz by bus or car. The small TI is on the main square (+33 5 59 54 20 14, www.sare.fr). Nearby is a cluster of hotels and the town church (which has an impressive interior, with arches over the gold-slathered altar and Basque-style balconies lining the nave). Reforms in the 18th century prohibited burials at or near Catholic churches, but Basque-style tombstones still surround the main church. At the far end of the square is the town's humble *fronton* (*pelota* court).

• *Leaving Sare, first follow signs for* toutes directions, *then St-Pée, and watch for the turnoff to...*

Ainhoa/Ainhoa

Ainhoa is a colorful, tidy, picturesque one-street town that sees fewer tourists (which is a good thing). Its chunks of old walls and

gates mingle with red-and-white half-timbered buildings. The 14th-century church—with a beautiful golden *retable* (screen behind the altar)—and the *fronton* share center stage. Parking is plentiful; resist the urge to turn off at the *fronton*—it's better to continue on for parking near the TI.

Ainhoa is also a popular starting point for hikes into the hills. For a spectacular village-and-valleys view, drive five minutes (or walk 90 sweaty minutes) up the steep dirt road to the Chapelle de Notre-Dame d'Aranazau ("d'Aubepine" in French). Start in the central parking lot directly across the main street from the church, then head straight uphill into the clouds. Follow signs for *oratoire*, then count the giant white crosses leading the way to the top. The chapel is occasionally closed, and cloudy days don't offer spectacular views, but the ethereal experience is worth the steep detour for drivers.

• *As you leave Ainhoa, you'll have to back-track the way you came in to find the road to...*

Espelette/Ezpeleta

Espelette won't let you forget that it's the capital of the region's AOC red peppers *(piments d'Espelette),* with strands of them dangling like good-luck charms from many houses and storefronts. After strolling the charming, cobbled center, head to the well-restored château and medieval tower of former local barons, which now houses

FRENCH BASQUE COUNTRY

the Town Hall, exhibition space, and the TI (+33 5 59 93 95 02, www.espelette.fr). Or wander downhill toward the pink *frontón*, following the *église* signs past houses constructed in the 1700s and a captivating stream, to find the town church. Climb up into the church balconies for some fancy views.

Sleeping and Eating: For a good regional meal, consider the **$$ Hôtel Euzkadi** restaurant,** with a *muy* Spanish ambience (closed Mon, Sept-June also closed Tue, 285 Karrika Nagusia, +33 5 59 93 91 88). The **$ hotel** has 27 rooms with modern touches and a swimming pool (air-con, elevator, www.hotel-restaurant-euzkadi.com).

• *From Espelette, if you have time, you can follow signs to* Cambo les Bains, *then* St-Jean-Pied-de-Port *(40 minutes, covered below).*

St-Jean-Pied-de-Port

Just five miles from the Spanish border, the walled town of St-Jean-Pied-de-Port (san-zhahn-pee-ay-duh-por) is the most popular vil-

lage in all the French Basque countryside (you may also see it labeled as Donibane Garazi, its Basque name). Traditionally, St-Jean-Pied-de-Port has been the final stopover in France for Santiago-bound pilgrims, who gather here to cross the Pyrenees together and continue their march through Spain. The scal-

lop shell of "St. Jacques" (French for "St. James") is etched on walls throughout the town.

About half the visitors to this town are pilgrims; the rest are mostly French tourists. Gift shops sell a strange combination of pilgrim gear (such as quick-drying shirts and shorts) and Basque souvenirs. This place is packed in the summer (so come early or late).

Tourist Information: The TI is on the main road along the outside of the walled old town (Mon-Sat 9:00-12:00 & 14:00-18:00, closed Sun except July-Aug Sun 10:00-13:00; +33 5 59 37 03 57, www.saintjeanpieddeport-paysbasque-tourisme.com). For Camino information, you'll do better at the Pilgrim Friends Office (described later). Ask the TI about weekly *pelota vasca* games (usually Mon at 17:00 at the *trinquet* court on Place du Trinquet).

Arrival in St-Jean-Pied-de-Port: Parking is ample and well signed from the main road. If arriving by **train,** exit the station to the left, then follow the first road to the right (Avenue Renaud). Signs for the TI and the Camino will lead you uphill to a gate in the city wall.

Sights in St-Jean-Pied-de-Port

There's little in the way of sightseeing here, other than pilgrim-spotting. But St-Jean-Pied-de-Port feels like the perfect "Welcome to the Camino" springboard for the upcoming journey. Many modern pilgrims begin their Camino in this traditional spot because of its easy train connection to Bayonne, and because—as its name implies ("St. John at the Foot of the Pass")—it offers a very challenging but rewarding first leg: up, over, and into Spain.

After passing through the gate in the city wall, follow Rue de France to the main drag, Rue de la Citadelle. Head left, uphill, and stop at #39, the **Pilgrim Friends Office** (Les Amis du Chemin de Saint-Jacques, daily 9:00-19:30, +33 5 59 37 05 09). This is where pilgrims check in before their long journey to Santiago.

For €2, pilgrims can buy the official credential (*credenciel* in French, *credencial* in Spanish) that they'll get stamped at each stop between here and Santiago to prove they walked the whole way and thereby earn their *compostela* certificate. Pilgrims also receive a warm welcome, lots of advice (like a handy chart breaking down the walk into 34 stages, with valuable distance and elevation information), and help finding a bunk (the well-traveled staff swears that no pilgrim ever goes without a bed in St-Jean-Pied-de-Port).

A few more steps up, on the left, you'll pass the skippable Bishop's Prison (Prison des Evêques). Continue on up to the **citadel,** dating from the mid-17th century—when this was a highly strategic location for keeping an eye on the easiest road over the Pyrenees between Spain and France. Although this stout fortress is not open to the public (as it houses a school), the grounds around it offer sweeping views over the French Basque countryside.

Now backtrack downhill toward the river. With rosy-pink buildings and ancient dates above doorways, this lane simply feels old. Notice lots of signs for *chambres* (rooms) and *refuges*—humble, hostel-like pilgrim bunkhouses. The **Notre-Dame Gate,** which was once a drawbridge, is straight ahead. Cross the old bridge over

The History of the Camino

The first person to undertake the Camino de Santiago was...Santiago himself. After the death of Christ, the apostles scattered to the corners of the earth to spread the Word of God. Supposedly, St. James went on a missionary trip from the Holy Land all the way to the northwest corner of Spain, which at that time really was the end of the Western world.

According to legend, St. James' remains were discovered in 813 in the town that would soon bear his name. This put Santiago de Compostela on the map, as one of three places—along with Rome and Jerusalem—where remains of apostles are known to be buried. In 951 the bishop of Le Puy in France walked to Santiago de Compostela to pay homage to the relics. As other pilgrims followed his example, the Camino de Santiago informally emerged. Then, in the 12th century, Pope Callistus II decreed that any person who walked to Santiago in a Holy Year, confessed their sins, and took Communion at the cathedral would be forgiven. This opportunity for a cheap indulgence made the Camino de Santiago one of the most important pilgrimages in the world.

It's probably no coincidence that St. James' remains were "discovered" and promoted just as the Reconquista was in full swing. The pope's decree helped to consolidate the Christians' hold over lands retaken from the Moors. Pilgrims were ideal candidates to repopulate and defend northern Spain. Many of those who made the journey to Santiago stuck around somewhere along the route (often because of privileges granted them by local rulers who needed help rebuilding). It became a self-sustaining little circle: Pilgrims came along the Camino, saw great sights, and decided to stay...to build even greater sights for the next pilgrims to enjoy.

The Christian monarchy designated an old Roman commercial road from France across northern Iberia as the "official" route, and soon churches, monasteries, hostels, hospitals, blacksmiths, and other pilgrims' services began to pop up. Religious-military orders such as the Knights of Santiago and the Knights Templar protected the route from bandits and fought alongside Christian armies against the Moorish resurgence, allowing the evolving Catholic state to gather strength in the safe haven created by the Camino.

In the Middle Ages, pilgrims came to Santiago from all over Europe. Many prominent figures embarked on the journey, including St. Francis of Assisi, Dutch painter Jan van Eyck, and the Wife of Bath in Chaucer's *Canterbury Tales.*

This steady flow of pilgrims from around Europe resulted in a rich exchange of knowledge, art, and architecture. Even today you'll find magnificent cathedrals along the Camino in cities such as Burgos and León, which incorporated and improved on the latest in cathedral design from France at that time.

By 1130 the trek was so popular that it prompted a French monk named Aimery Picaud to pen (likely with the help of some ghostwriters) a chronicle of his journey, including tips on where to eat, where to stay, the best way to get from place to place, and how to pack light and use a money belt. This Codex Calixtinus (Latin for "Camino Through the Back Door") was the world's first guidebook—the great-great-granddaddy of the one you're holding right now.

In the age of Columbus, the Renaissance, and the Reformation, interest in the Camino dropped way off. When the Moors were finally defeated in 1492, the significance of Reconquista icon St. James fell by the wayside. The discovery of the New World in the same year led both the Church and the monarchy to turn their attention across the Atlantic, and the pilgrimage began to wane. That was followed by a century of religious wars pitting Catholics against Protestants, which also distracted potential pilgrims. Feeling threatened by the pirate Francis Drake (not considered "sir" in Spain), the church hid the remains of St. James so thoroughly that they were lost for generations. Meanwhile, the rise of humanism during the Renaissance diminished the mystique of the pilgrimage. For the next centuries, and as recently as a few decades ago, only a few hardy souls followed the route.

In the late 1960s, a handful of parish priests along the Camino began working to recover the route, establishing associations of "friends of the Camino" that would eventually agree on a path and mark it. They received help from none other than Generalísimo Francisco Franco, who decided that Catholicism and nationalism went hand-in-hand. By reviving the Camino, he reasoned, Spain was assured to relive its most glorious days. In 1982, and again in 1989, Pope John Paul II visited Santiago de Compostela, reminding the world of the town's historic significance. In 1987 the European Union designated the Camino as Europe's first Cultural Itinerary. And after the success of the 1992 Expo in Sevilla, the Galician government decided to pour funds into reviving the tradition for the Holy Year in 1993.

The plan worked, and now—aided by European Union funding—the route has enjoyed a huge renaissance of interest, with more than 200,000 pilgrims each year trekking to Santiago. Cyclists and horse riders are now joining hikers on the journey, and these days it's "in" to follow the seashells to Santiago.

FRENCH BASQUE COUNTRY

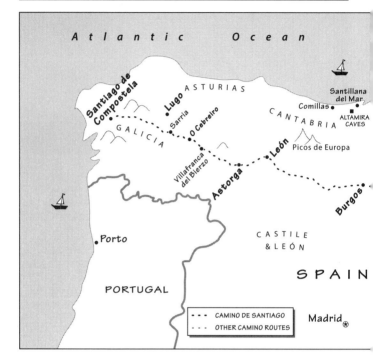

the Nive River (the same one that winds up in Bayonne) and head up **Rue d'Espagne** to restaurant row—Rue d'Uhart—for a break before your Camino begins.

Sleeping and Eating in St-Jean-Pied-de-Port

Sleeping: Lots of humble pilgrim lodgings line the main drag, Rue de la Citadelle. If you're looking for a bit more comfort, consider these options (stars are based on the French rating system).

$ Hotel Ramuntcho** is the only real hotel option in the old town, located partway up Rue de la Citadelle. Its 18 rooms above a restaurant are straightforward but modern (buffet breakfast, 1 Rue de France, +33 5 59 37 03 91, www.hotel-ramuntcho.com, hotel.ramuntcho@wanadoo.fr).

$ Itzalpea,** a café and teahouse, rents five rooms along the main road just outside the old town (closed Sat off-season, air-con, 5 Place du Trinquet, +33 5 59 37 03 66, www.hotel-itzalpea.com, itzalpea@wanadoo.fr).

$ Chambres Chez l'Habitant has five old-fashioned, pilgrim-perfect rooms along the main drag. Welcoming Maria and Jean

Pierre speak limited English, but their daughter can help translate (15 Rue de la Citadelle, +33 5 59 37 05 83).

Eating: Tourists, pilgrims, and locals alike find plenty of **$$** places to eat along Rue de la Citadelle (heading up to the citadel), Rue du Trinquet (the main traffic street into town), and Rue d'Uhart. Consider **Café Navarre** (1 Place Juan de Huarte, +33 5 59 37 01 67) or **Cafe Ttipia** (2 Place Charles Floquet, +33 5 59 37 11 96), both very popular with locals. If you're lucky enough to land here on a Monday morning, shop at the **weekly market,** where farmers, cheesemakers, and winemakers bring their products from the countryside.

St-Jean-Pied-de-Port Connections

A scenic train conveniently links St-Jean-Pied-de-Port to **Bayonne** (4/day, 1 hour) and from there to **St-Jean-de-Luz** (about 45 minutes beyond Bayonne, www.sncf.fr). It's about a 1.5-hour drive to St-Jean-de-Luz. There is also limited bus service from St-Jean-Pied-de-Port to **Pamplona** (bus stop at Place Juan de Huarte near Hôtel Les Remparts, 2/day, 1.5 hours, run by the Spanish line Alsa, www.alsa.es). NavarVIP offers taxi service to Pamplona for about €100 (+34 948 102 100, www.navarvip.com, Luis).

PRACTICALITIES

This section covers just the basics on traveling in the destinations in this book (for much more information, see *Rick Steves Spain*). You can find free advice on specific topics at RickSteves.com/tips.

MONEY

Spain and France use the euro currency: 1 euro (€) = about $1.20. To convert prices in euros to dollars, add about 20 percent: €20 = about $24, €50 = about $60. (Check www.oanda.com for the latest exchange rates.)

The standard way for travelers to get euros is to withdraw money from an ATM (known as a *cajero automático* in Spain and a *distributeur* in France) using a debit or credit card, ideally with a Visa or MasterCard logo.

Before departing, call your bank or credit-card company: Confirm that your card(s) will work overseas, ask about international transaction fees, and alert them that you'll be making withdrawals in Europe. Also ask for the PIN number for your credit card—you may need it for Europe's "chip-and-PIN" payment machines. Allow time for your bank to mail your PIN to you.

European cards use chip-and-PIN technology; most chip cards issued in the US instead require a signature. European card readers may generate a receipt for you to sign— or prompt you to enter your PIN (so it's good to know it). US credit cards may not work at some self-service payment machines (transit-ticket kiosks, parking kiosks, etc.). If your card won't work, look for a cashier who can process the transaction manually—or pay in cash.

"Tap to pay" cards and smartphone payment apps work in Europe just as they do in the US, and sidestep chip-and-PIN compatibility issues.

To keep your cash, cards, and other valuables safe, wear a money belt.

Dynamic Currency Conversion: If merchants offer to convert your purchase price into dollars (called dynamic currency conversion, or DCC), refuse this "service." You'll pay extra for the expensive convenience of seeing your charge in dollars. If an ATM offers to "lock in" your conversion rate, choose "proceed without conversion." Other prompts might state, "You can be charged in dollars: Press YES for dollars, NO for euros." Always choose the local currency.

STAYING CONNECTED

The simplest solution is to bring your own device—mobile phone, tablet, or laptop—and use it just as you would at home (following the money-saving tips below). For more on phoning, see RickSteves.com/phoning. For a one-hour talk covering tech issues for travelers, see RickSteves.com/mobile-travel-skills.

To Call from a US Phone: Phone numbers in this book are presented exactly as you would dial them from a US mobile phone. For international access, press and hold the 0 key until you get a + sign, then dial the country code (34 for Spain, 33 for France) and phone number (omitting the initial zero in France). To dial from a US landline, replace + with 011 (US/Canada international access code).

From a European Landline: Replace + with 0 (Europe international access code), then dial the country code (34 for Spain, 33 for France) and phone number (omitting the initial zero in France).

Within Spain or France: To place a domestic call (from a Spanish or French landline or mobile), drop the +34 or +33 from the phone number printed in this book. For France, retain the initial 0.

Tips: If you bring your mobile phone, consider getting an international plan; most providers offer a simple bundle that includes calling, messaging, and data.

Use Wi-Fi whenever possible. Most hotels and many cafés offer free Wi-Fi, and you may also find it at tourist information offices (TIs), major museums, and public-transit hubs. With Wi-Fi you can use your phone or tablet to make free or low-cost calls via a calling app such as Skype, WhatsApp, FaceTime, or Google Hangouts. When you need to get online but can't find Wi-Fi, turn on your cellular network (or turn off airplane mode) just long enough for the task at hand.

Most hotels charge a fee for placing calls—ask for rates before you dial. You can use a prepaid international phone card (called a *tarjeta telefónica con código* in Spain and a *carte à code* in France, usu-

Sleep Code

Hotels in this book are categorized according to the average price of a standard double room without breakfast in high season.

Code		Spain	France
$$$$	Splurge	Most rooms over €170	Most rooms over €250
$$$	Pricier	€130-170	€190-250
$$	Moderate	€90-130	€130-190
$	Budget	€50-90	€70-130
¢	Backpacker	Under €50	Under €70

Unless otherwise noted, credit cards are accepted, hotel staff speak basic English, and free Wi-Fi is available. Comparison-shop by checking prices at several hotels (on each hotel's own website, on a booking site, or by email). For the best deal, *book directly with the hotel.* Ask for a discount if paying in cash; if the listing includes **RS%**, request a Rick Steves discount.

ally available at newsstands, tobacco shops, and train stations) to call out from your hotel.

SLEEPING

I've categorized my recommended accommodations based on price, indicated with a dollar-sign rating (see sidebar). I recommend reserving rooms in advance, particularly during peak season. Once your dates are set, check the specific price for your preferred stay at several hotels. You can do this either by comparing prices on Hotels.com or Booking.com, or by checking the hotels' own websites. To get the best deal, contact my family-run hotels directly by phone or email. When you go direct, the owner avoids the commission paid to booking sites, giving them wiggle room to offer you a discount, a nicer room, or free breakfast. If you prefer to book online, it's to your advantage to use the hotel's website.

For complicated requests, send an email with the following information: number and type of rooms; number of nights; arrival date; departure date; any special needs; and applicable discounts (such as a Rick Steves discount, cash discount, or promotional rate). Use the European style for writing dates: day/month/year.

The French have a simple hotel-rating system based on amenities (from zero through five stars, indicated in this book's French hotel listings by * through *****).

In general, hotel prices can soften if you do any of the following: offer to pay cash, stay at least three nights, or travel off-season.

PRACTICALITIES

Restaurant Code

Eateries in this book are categorized according to the average cost of a typical main course. Drinks, desserts, and splurge items can raise the price considerably.

Code		Spain	France
$$$$	Splurge	Most main courses over €25	Most main courses over €30
$$$	Pricier	€18-25	€25-30
$$	Moderate	€12-18	€15-25
$	Budget	Under €12	Under €15

In the Basque Country, takeout food is **$**; a basic tapas bar or no-frills sit-down eatery is **$$**; a casual but more upscale tapas bar or restaurant is **$$$**; and a swanky splurge is **$$$$**.

Hoteliers in Spain are encouraged to quote prices with the IVA tax (value-added tax) included—but it's smart to ask when you book your room.

Room rates are especially volatile at hotels that use "dynamic pricing" to set rates. Prices can skyrocket during festivals and conventions, while business hotels can have deep discounts on weekends when demand plummets. Of the many hotels I recommend, it's difficult to say which will be the best value on a given day—until you do your homework.

EATING

I've categorized my recommended eateries in Spain and France based on the average price of a typical main course, indicated with a dollar-sign rating (see sidebar).

Eating in Spain: By our standards, Spaniards eat late, having lunch—their biggest meal of the day—around 13:00-16:00, and dinner starting about 21:00. At restaurants, you can dine with tourists at 20:00, or with Spaniards if you wait until later.

For a fun early dinner at a bar, build a light meal out of tapas—small appetizer-sized portions of seafood, salads, meat-filled pastries, deep-fried tasties, and so on. Many of these are displayed behind glass, and you can point to what you want. Tapas typically cost around €4. While the smaller "tapa" size (which comes on a saucer-size plate) is handiest for maximum tasting opportunities, many bars sell only larger sizes: the *ración* (full portion, on a dinner plate) and *media-ración* (half-size portion). *Jamón* (hah-MOHN), an air-dried ham similar to prosciutto, is a Spanish staple. Other key terms include *bocadillo* (baguette sandwich), *frito* (fried), *a la plancha* (grilled), *queso* (cheese), *tortilla* (omelet), and *surtido* (assortment).

Many bars have three price tiers, which should be clearly posted: It's cheapest to eat or drink while standing at the bar (*barra*), slightly more to sit at a table inside (*mesa* or *salón*), and most expensive to sit outside *(terraza)*. Wherever you are, be assertive or you'll never be served. *Por favor* (please) grabs the attention of the server or bartender.

If you're having tapas, don't worry about paying as you go (the bartender keeps track). When you're ready to leave, ask for the bill: *"¿La cuenta?"*

Tipping in Spain: To tip for a few tapas, round up to the nearest euro. At restaurants with table service, if a service charge is included in the bill, add about 5 percent; if it's not, leave 10 percent. If you're sampling tapas at a counter, there's no need to tip (though you can round up the bill).

Eating in France: Restaurants serve lunch from about 11:30 to 14:00. They usually open for dinner at 19:00 and are typically most crowded around 20:30. Cafés and brasseries serve throughout the day. They generally have more limited menus than restaurants, but offer more budget options, including salads, sandwiches, omelets, *plats du jour*, and more. Check the price list first, which by law must be posted prominently. There are two sets of prices: You'll pay more for the same drink if you're seated at a table *(salle)* than if you're seated at the bar or counter *(comptoir)*.

In France, an entrée is the first course, and *le plat* or *le plat du jour* is the main course with vegetables. At restaurants, it's common to order *une entrée* and *un plat*, or *un plat* and *un dessert*, or just *un plat*. If you ask for the *menu* (muh-noo), you'll get a fixed-price meal—usually your choice of three courses (soup, appetizer, or salad; main course with vegetables; and cheese course or dessert). Drinks are extra. Ask for *la carte* (lah kart) if you want to see a menu and order à la carte, like the locals do. Request the waiter's help in deciphering the French.

Tipping in France: At French cafés and restaurants, a 12-15 percent service charge is always included in the price of what you order (*service compris* or *prix net*), but you won't see it listed on your bill. Most French tip a little or not at all. But if you feel the service was good, tip about 5 percent; and maybe 10 percent for terrific service.

TRANSPORTATION

By Train: To research train schedules, visit Germany's excellent all-Europe website (www.bahn.com), Spain's Renfe (www.renfe.com), or France's SNCF (http://en.voyages-sncf.com).

In Spain, you can buy tickets at the train station, but you'll pay a five percent service fee at the ticket window. Many travelers prefer to buy tickets at travel agencies in Spain, because there's a smaller language barrier than at the station. You can also buy tickets online (at www.renfe.com). Be aware that the Renfe website often rejects US credit cards—use PayPal; or from the US try Raileurope.com and Petrabax.com (expect a small fee from either), or use the European vendor Trainline.eu. Since trains can sell out, it's smart to buy your tickets at least a day in advance—even for short rides.

In France, you can buy train tickets in person at any train station, either from a staffed ticket window or from a machine. The ticket machines at most stations are great timesavers when ticket counter lines are long. While most machines accept American chip cards if you know the PIN code, be prepared with euro coins and bills just in case.

The fast, reserved TGV trains get booked up, so buy well ahead for any TGV you cannot afford to miss. Tickets go on sale as far as four months in advance, with a wide range of prices. Note that US credit cards often don't work on SNCF websites, but American customers can order through a US agency, such as RickSteves.com/rail, which offers both etickets and home delivery, or European vendor Trainline.eu.

At major stations you'll need to scan your ticket at turnstiles to access the tracks. Smaller stations still use the old system of validating your ticket in yellow machines near the platform or waiting area. Print-at-home tickets and etickets don't require validation.

By Bus: In Spain and France, buses pick up where the trains don't go, reaching even small villages. In Spain, routes are operated by various competing companies, so it can be tricky to pin down schedules (check with local bus stations, tourist info offices, or the aggregator website Movelia.es). In France, for cheap long-distance bus fares, check out Blablabus (www.blablabus.com) and Flixbus (www.flixbus.com).

By Car: It's cheaper to arrange most car rentals from the US. If you're planning a multicountry itinerary by car, be aware of high international drop-off fees. For tips on your insurance options, see RickSteves.com/cdw. In Spain, you're technically required to have an International Driving Permit (IDP), available at your local AAA office ($20 plus two passport-type photos, www.aaa.com).

For navigation, the mapping app on your phone works fine for Europe's roads. To save on data, most apps allow you to download maps for offline use. Some apps—including Google Maps—also have offline route directions, but you'll need mobile data access for current traffic.

Superhighways come with tolls, but save lots of time; in France, pay cash (coins or bills under €50) at toll booths, since some

US credit cards won't work. A car is a worthless headache in cities—park it safely (get tips from your hotel). As break-ins are common, be sure valuables are out of sight and locked in the trunk, or even better, with you or in your hotel room.

Local road etiquette is similar to that in the US. Ask your car-rental company about the rules of the road, or check the US State Department website (www.travel.state.gov, search for Spain or France in the "Country Information" box, then select "Travel and Transportation").

By Plane: Consider covering long distances on a budget flight, which can be cheaper than a train or bus ride. Check the cost of a flight on one of Europe's airlines, whether a major carrier or a no-frills outfit like EasyJet or Ryanair. Kayak is the top site for flights to and within Europe, easy-to-use Google Flights has price alerts, and Skyscanner includes many inexpensive flights within Europe.

HELPFUL HINTS

Travel Advisories: For updated health and safety conditions, including any restrictions for your destination, consult the US State Department's international travel website (www.travel.state.gov).

Emergency and Medical Help: For any emergency service—ambulance, police, or fire—call 112 from a mobile phone or landline. Operators, who in most countries speak English, will deal with your request or route you to the right emergency service. If you get sick, do as the locals do and go to a pharmacist for advice. Or ask at your hotel for help—they'll know of the nearest medical and emergency services.

For **passport problems,** contact the **US Embassy** (Madrid—by appointment only, dial +34 915 872 200, https://es.usembassy.gov; Paris—dial +33 1 43 12 22 22, https://fr.usembassy.gov) or the **Canadian Embassy** (Madrid—by appointment only, dial +34 913 828 400, www.espana.gc.ca; Paris—dial +33 1 44 43 29 00, www.canadainternational.gc.ca).

ETIAS Registration: Beginning in late 2021, US and Canadian citizens may be required to register online with the European Travel Information and Authorization System (ETIAS) before entering certain European countries (quick and easy process, $8 fee, valid 3 years, www.etiasvisa.com).

Theft or Loss: Spain and France have particularly hardworking pickpockets—wear a money belt. Assume beggars are pickpockets and any scuffle is simply a distraction by a team of thieves. If you stop for any commotion or show, put your hands in your pockets before someone else does.

To replace a passport, you'll need to go in person to an embassy (see above). Cancel and replace your credit and debit cards by calling these 24-hour US numbers with a mobile phone: Visa (dial +1-303-967-1096), MasterCard (dial +1-636-722-7111), and American Express (dial +1-336-393-1111). From a landline, you can call these US numbers collect by going through a local operator. File a police report either on the spot or within a day or two; it's required if you submit an insurance claim for lost or stolen rail passes or travel gear, and it can help with replacing your passport or credit and debit cards. For more information, see RickSteves.com/help.

Time: Spain and France use the 24-hour clock. It's the same through 12:00 noon, then keep going: 13:00, 14:00, and so on. Like most of continental Europe, Spain and France are six/nine hours ahead of the East/West Coasts of the US.

Business Hours: In Spain, many shops are generally open Monday-Friday 9:00-14:00 and 17:00-21:00, open Saturday morning, and closed on Sunday. In rural France, most shops are open Monday-Saturday 10:00–12:00 and 14:00–19:00, closed on Sunday and Monday mornings. In more touristy places in either country, shops can be open throughout the day (without a lunch closure) and on Sunday.

Sights: Major attractions can be swamped with visitors; carefully read and follow this book's crowd-beating tips (visit popular sights very early or very late, or—where possible—reserve ahead). Opening and closing hours of sights can change unexpectedly; confirm the latest times on their websites or at the local tourist information office. At many churches, a modest dress code is encouraged and sometimes required (no bare shoulders or shorts).

Holidays and Festivals: Spain and France celebrate many holidays, which can close sights and attract crowds (book hotel rooms ahead). For more on holidays and festivals in Spain, check www.spain.info; for France, check http://us.france.fr. For a simple list showing major—though not all—events, see RickSteves.com/festivals.

Numbers and Stumblers: What Americans call the second floor of a building is the first floor in Europe. Europeans write dates as day/month/year, so Christmas 2021 is 25/12/21. Commas are decimal points and vice versa—a dollar and a half is 1,50, and there are 5.280 feet in a mile. Spain and France use the metric system: A kilogram is 2.2 pounds; a liter is about a quart; and a kilometer is six-tenths of a mile.

RESOURCES FROM RICK STEVES

This Snapshot guide, excerpted from my latest edition of *Rick Steves Spain*, is one of many titles in my series of guidebooks on European travel. I also produce a public television series, *Rick Steves' Europe*, and a public radio show, *Travel with Rick Steves*. My free online video library, Rick Steves Classroom Europe, offers a searchable database of short video clips on European history, culture, and geography (Classroom.RickSteves.com). My website, RickSteves. com, offers free travel information, a forum for travelers' comments, guidebook updates, my travel blog, an online travel store, and information on European rail passes and our tours of Europe. If you're bringing a mobile device, you can download my free Rick Steves Audio Europe app that features dozens of free, self-guided audio tours of the top sights in Europe, plus radio shows and travel interviews about Spain and France. For more information, see RickSteves.com/audioeurope. You can also follow me on Facebook, Twitter, and Instagram.

ADDITIONAL RESOURCES

Tourist Information: www.spain.info and http://us.france.fr
Passports and Red Tape: www.travel.state.gov
Packing List: www.ricksteves.com/packing
Travel Insurance Tips: www.ricksteves.com/insurance
Cheap Flights: www.kayak.com or www.google.com/flights
Airplane Carry-on Restrictions: www.tsa.gov/travelers
Updates for This Book: www.ricksteves.com/update

HOW WAS YOUR TRIP?

To share your tips, concerns, and discoveries after using this book, please fill out the survey at RickSteves.com/feedback. Thanks in advance—it helps a lot.

Spanish Survival Phrases

English	Spanish	Pronunciation
Good day.	*Buenos días.*	**bweh**-nohs **dee**-ahs
Do you speak English?	*¿Habla usted inglés?*	ah-blah oo-**stehd** een-**glays**
Yes. / No.	*Sí. / No.*	see / noh
I (don't) understand.	*(No) comprendo.*	(noh) kohm-**prehn**-doh
Please.	*Por favor.*	por fah-**bor**
Thank you.	*Gracias.*	**grah**-thee-ahs
I'm sorry.	*Lo siento.*	loh see-**ehn**-toh
Excuse me.	*Perdone.*	pehr-**doh**-nay
(No) problem.	*(No) problema.*	(noh) proh-**bleh**-mah
Good.	*Bueno.*	**bweh**-noh
Goodbye.	*Adiós.*	ah-dee-**ohs**
OK.	*Vale.*	**bah**-lay
one / two	*uno / dos*	**oo**-noh / dohs
three / four	*tres / cuatro*	trehs / **kwah**-troh
five / six	*cinco / seis*	**theen**-koh / says
seven / eight	*siete / ocho*	see-**eh**-tay / **oh**-choh
nine / ten	*nueve / diez*	**nweh**-bay / dee-**ehth**
How much is it?	*¿Cuánto cuesta?*	**kwahn**-toh **kweh**-stah
Write it?	*¿Me lo escribe?*	may loh ehs-**skree**-bay
Is it free?	*¿Es gratis?*	ehs **grah**-tees
Is it included?	*¿Está incluido?*	eh-**stah** een-kloo-**ee**-doh
Where can I buy / find...?	*¿Dónde puedo comprar / encontrar...?*	**dohn**-day **pweh**-doh kohm-**prar** / ehn-kohn-**trar**
I'd like / We'd like...	*Me gustaría / Nos gustaría...*	may goo-stah-**ree**-ah / nohs goo-stah-**ree**-ah
...a room.	*...una habitación.*	**oo**-nah ah-bee-tah-thee-**ohn**
...a ticket to ___.	*...un billete para ___.*	oon bee-**yeh**-tay **pah**-rah ___
Is it possible?	*¿Es posible?*	ehs poh-**see**-blay
Where is...?	*¿Dónde está...?*	**dohn**-day eh-**stah**
...the train station	*...la estación de trenes*	lah eh-stah-thee-**ohn** day **treh**-nehs
...the bus station	*...la estación de autobuses*	lah eh-stah-thee-**ohn** day ow-toh-**boo**-sehs
...the tourist information office	*...la oficina de turismo*	lah oh-fee-**thee**-nah day too-**rees**-moh
Where are the toilets?	*¿Dónde están los servicios?*	**dohn**-day eh-**stahn** lohs sehr-**bee**-thee-ohs
men	*hombres, caballeros*	**ohm**-brehs, kah-bah-**yeh**-rohs
women	*mujeres, damas*	moo-**heh**-rehs, **dah**-mahs
left / right	*izquierda / derecha*	eeth-kee-**ehr**-dah / deh-**reh**-chah
straight	*derecho*	deh-**reh**-choh
When do you open / close?	*¿A qué hora abren / cierran?*	ah kay **oh**-rah **ah**-brehn / thee-**ehr**-ahn
At what time?	*¿A qué hora?*	ah kay **oh**-rah
Just a moment.	*Un momento.*	oon moh-**mehn**-toh
now / soon / later	*ahora / pronto / más tarde*	ah-**oh**-rah / **prohn**-toh / mahs **tar**-day
today / tomorrow	*hoy / mañana*	oy / mahn-**yah**-nah

In a Spanish Restaurant

English	Spanish	Pronunciation
I'd like / We'd like...	Me gustaría / Nos gustaría...	may goo-stah-**ree**-ah / nohs goo-stah-**ree**-ah
...to reserve...	...reservar...	reh-sehr-**bar**
...a table for one / two.	...una mesa para uno / dos.	**oo**-nah meh-sah **pah**-rah **oo**-noh / dohs
Non-smoking.	No fumador.	noh foo-mah-**dohr**
Is this table free?	¿Está esta mesa libre?	eh-**stah** eh-stah meh-sah **lee**-bray
The menu (in English), please.	La carta (en inglés), por favor.	lah **kar**-tah (ehn een-**glays**) por fah-**bor**
service (not) included	servicio (no) incluido	sehr-**bee**-thee-oh (noh) een-kloo-**ee**-doh
cover charge	precio de entrada	**preh**-thee-oh day ehn-**trah**-dah
to go	para llevar	**pah**-rah yeh-**bar**
with / without	con / sin	kohn / seen
and / or	y / o	ee / oh
menu (of the day)	menú (del día)	meh-**noo** (dehl **dee**-ah)
specialty of the house	especialidad de la casa	eh-speh-thee-ah-lee-**dahd** day lah **kah**-sah
tourist menu	menú turístico	meh-**noo** too-**ree**-stee-koh
combination plate	plato combinado	**plah**-toh kohm-bee-**nah**-doh
appetizers	tapas	**tah**-pahs
bread	pan	pahn
cheese	queso	**keh**-soh
sandwich	bocadillo	boh-kah-**dee**-yoh
soup	sopa	**soh**-pah
salad	ensalada	ehn-sah-**lah**-dah
meat	carne	**kar**-nay
poultry	aves	**ah**-behs
fish	pescado	peh-**skah**-doh
seafood	marisco	mah-**ree**-skoh
fruit	fruta	**froo**-tah
vegetables	verduras	behr-**doo**-rahs
dessert	postre	**poh**-stray
tap water	agua del grifo	**ah**-gwah dehl **gree**-foh
mineral water	agua mineral	**ah**-gwah mee-neh-**rahl**
milk	leche	**leh**-chay
(orange) juice	zumo (de naranja)	**thoo**-moh (day nah-**rahn**-hah)
coffee	café	kah-**fay**
tea	té	tay
wine	vino	**bee**-noh
red / white	tinto / blanco	**teen**-toh / **blahn**-koh
glass / bottle	vaso / botella	**bah**-soh / boh-**teh**-yah
beer	cerveza	thehr-**beh**-thah
Cheers!	¡Salud!	sah-**lood**
More. / Another.	Más. / Otro.	mahs / **oh**-troh
The same.	El mismo.	ehl **mees**-moh
The bill, please.	La cuenta, por favor.	lah **kwehn**-tah por fah-**bor**
tip	propina	proh-**pee**-nah
Delicious!	¡Delicioso!	deh-lee-thee-**oh**-soh

For hundreds more pages of survival phrases for your trip to Spain, check out *Rick Steves Spanish Phrase Book*.

French Survival Phrases

When using the phonetics, try to nasalize the <u>n</u> sound.

English	French	Pronunciation
Good day.	*Bonjour.*	boh<u>n</u>-zhoor
Mrs. / Mr.	*Madame / Monsieur*	mah-dahm / muhs-yuh
Do you speak English?	*Parlez-vous anglais?*	par-lay-voo ah<u>n</u>-glay
Yes. / No.	*Oui. / Non.*	wee / noh<u>n</u>
I understand.	*Je comprends.*	zhuh koh<u>n</u>-prah<u>n</u>
I don't understand.	*Je ne comprends pas.*	zhuh nuh koh<u>n</u>-prah<u>n</u> pah
Please.	*S'il vous plaît.*	see voo play
Thank you.	*Merci.*	mehr-see
I'm sorry.	*Désolé.*	day-zoh-lay
Excuse me.	*Pardon.*	par-doh<u>n</u>
(No) problem.	*(Pas de) problème.*	(pah duh) proh-blehm
It's good.	*C'est bon.*	say boh<u>n</u>
Goodbye.	*Au revoir.*	oh ruh-vwahr
one / two / three	*un / deux / trois*	uh<u>n</u> / duh / trwah
four / five / six	*quatre / cinq / six*	kah-truh / sa<u>n</u>k / sees
seven / eight	*sept / huit*	seht / weet
nine / ten	*neuf / dix*	nuhf / dees
How much is it?	*Combien?*	koh<u>n</u>-bee-a<u>n</u>
Write it?	*Ecrivez?*	ay-kree-vay
Is it free?	*C'est gratuit?*	say grah-twee
Included?	*Inclus?*	a<u>n</u>-klew
Where can I buy / find...?	*Où puis-je acheter / trouver...?*	oo pwee-zhuh ah-shuh-tay / troo-vay
I'd like / We'd like...	*Je voudrais / Nous voudrions...*	zhuh voo-dray / noo voo-dree-oh<u>n</u>
...a room.	*...une chambre.*	ewn shah<u>n</u>-bruh
...a ticket to ___.	*...un billet pour ___.*	uh<u>n</u> bee-yay poor ___
Is it possible?	*C'est possible?*	say poh-see-bluh
Where is...?	*Où est...?*	oo ay
...the train station	*...la gare*	lah gar
...the bus station	*...la gare routière*	lah gar root-yehr
...tourist information	*...l'office du tourisme*	loh-fees dew too-reez-muh
Where are the toilets?	*Où sont les toilettes?*	oo soh<u>n</u> lay twah-leht
men	*hommes*	ohm
women	*dames*	dahm
left / right	*à gauche / à droite*	ah gohsh / ah drwaht
straight	*tout droit*	too drwah
pull / push	*tirez / poussez*	tee-ray / poo-say
When does this open / close?	*Ça ouvre / ferme à quelle heure?*	sah oo-vruh / fehrm ah kehl ur
At what time?	*À quelle heure?*	ah kehl ur
Just a moment.	*Un moment.*	uh<u>n</u> moh-mah<u>n</u>
now / soon / later	*maintenant / bientôt / plus tard*	ma<u>n</u>-tuh-nah<u>n</u> / bee-a<u>n</u>-toh / plew tar
today / tomorrow	*aujourd'hui / demain*	oh-zhoor-dwee / duh-ma<u>n</u>

In a French Restaurant

English	French	Pronunciation
I'd like / We'd like...	Je voudrais / Nous voudrions...	zhuh voo-dray / noo voo-dree-oh<u>n</u>
...to reserve...	...réserver...	ray-zehr-vay
...a table for one / two.	...une table pour un / deux.	ewn tah-bluh poor uh<u>n</u> / duh
Is this seat free?	C'est libre?	say lee-bruh
The menu (in English), please.	La carte (en anglais), s'il vous plaît.	lah kart (ahn ah<u>n</u>-glay) see voo play
service (not) included	service (non) compris	sehr-vees (noh<u>n</u>) koh<u>n</u>-pree
to go	à emporter	ah ah<u>n</u>-por-tay
with / without	avec / sans	ah-vehk / sah<u>n</u>
and / or	et / ou	ay / oo
special of the day	plat du jour	plah dew zhoor
specialty of the house	spécialité de la maison	spay-see-ah-lee-tay duh lah may-zoh<u>n</u>
appetizers	hors d'oeuvre	or duh-vruh
first course (soup, salad)	entrée	ah<u>n</u>-tray
main course (meat, fish)	plat principal	plah pra<u>n</u>-see-pahl
bread	pain	pa<u>n</u>
cheese	fromage	froh-mahzh
sandwich	sandwich	sahnd-weech
soup	soupe	soop
salad	salade	sah-lahd
meat	viande	vee-ahnd
chicken	poulet	poo-lay
fish	poisson	pwah-soh<u>n</u>
seafood	fruits de mer	frwee duh mehr
fruit	fruit	frwee
vegetables	légumes	lay-gewm
dessert	dessert	day-sehr
mineral water	eau minérale	oh mee-nay-rahl
tap water	l'eau du robinet	loh dew roh-bee-nay
milk	lait	lay
(orange) juice	jus (d'orange)	zhew (doh-rah<u>n</u>zh)
coffee / tea	café / thé	kah-fay / tay
wine	vin	va<u>n</u>
red / white	rouge / blanc	roozh / blah<u>n</u>
glass / bottle	verre / bouteille	vehr / boo-tay
beer	bière	bee-ehr
Cheers!	Santé!	sah<u>n</u>-tay
More. / Another.	Plus. / Un autre.	plew / uhn oh-truh
The same.	La même chose.	lah mehm shohz
The bill, please.	L'addition, s'il vous plaît.	lah-dee-see-oh<u>n</u> see voo play
Do you accept credit cards?	Vous prenez les cartes?	voo pruh-nay lay kart
tip	pourboire	poor-bwahr
Delicious!	Délicieux!	day-lees-yuh

For more user-friendly French phrases, check out *Rick Steves French Phrase Book* or *Rick Steves French, Italian & German Phrase Book*.

INDEX

INDEX

INDEX

Explore Europe

At ricksteves.com you can browse through thousands of articles, videos, photos and radio interviews, plus find a wealth of money-saving travel tips for planning your dream trip. And with our mobile-friendly website, you can easily access all this great travel information anywhere you go.

TV Shows

Preview the places you'll visit by watching entire half-hour episodes of *Rick Steves' Europe* (choose from all 100 shows) on-demand, for free.

ricksteves.com

your travel dreams into affordable reality

Radio Interviews

Enjoy ready access to Rick's vast library of radio interviews covering travel tips and cultural insights that relate specifically to your Europe travel plans.

Travel Forums

Learn, ask, share! Our online community of savvy travelers is a great resource for first-time travelers to Europe, as well as seasoned pros.

Travel News

Subscribe to our free Travel News e-newsletter, and get monthly updates from Rick on what's happening in Europe.

Classroom Europe

Check out our free resource for educators with 400+ short video clips from the *Rick Steves' Europe* TV show.

Audio Europe™

Gear up for your next adventure at ricksteves.com

Light Luggage

Pack light and right with Rick Steves' affordable, custom-designed rolling carry-on bags, backpacks, day packs and shoulder bags.

Accessories

From packing cubes to moneybelts and beyond, Rick has personally selected the travel goodies that will help your trip go smoother.

Shop at ricksteves.com

Save time and energy

This guidebook is your independent-travel toolkit. But for all it delivers, it's still up to you to devote the time and energy it takes to manage the preparation and logistics that are essential for a happy trip. If that's a hassle, there's a solution.

Rick Steves Tours

A Rick Steves tour takes you to Europe's most interesting places with great

guides and small groups. We follow Rick's favorite itineraries, ride in comfy buses, stay in family-run hotels, and bring you intimately close to the Europe you've traveled so far to see. Most importantly, we take away the logistical headaches so you can focus on the fun.

Join the fun

This year we'll take thousands of free-spirited travelers—nearly half of them repeat customers— along with us on 50 different itineraries, from Athens to Istanbul. Is a Rick Steves tour the right fit for your travel dreams?

Find out at ricksteves.com, where you can also check seat availability and sign up. Europe is best experienced with happy travel partners. We hope you can join us.

BEST OF GUIDES

Full-color guides in an easy-to-scan format. Focused on top sights and experiences in the most popular European destinations

Best of England
Best of Europe
Best of France
Best of Germany
Best of Ireland
Best of Italy
Best of Scotland
Best of Spain

COMPREHENSIVE GUIDES

City, country, and regional guides printed on Bible-thin paper. Packed with detailed coverage for a multi-week trip exploring iconic sights and venturing off the beaten path

Amsterdam & the Netherlands
Barcelona
Belgium: Bruges, Brussels, Antwerp & Ghent
Berlin
Budapest
Croatia & Slovenia
Eastern Europe
England
Florence & Tuscany
France
Germany
Great Britain
Greece: Athens & the Peloponnese
Iceland
Ireland
Istanbul
Italy
London
Paris
Portugal
Prague & the Czech Republic
Provence & the French Riviera
Rome
Scandinavia
Scotland
Sicily
Spain
Switzerland
Venice
Vienna, Salzburg & Tirol

THE BEST OF ROME

me, Italy's capital, is studded with
man remnants and floodlit-fountain
ares. From the Vatican to the Colos-
m, with crazy traffic in between, Rome
nderful, huge, and exhausting. The
ds, the heat, and the weighty history

of the Eternal City where Caesars walked
can make tourists wilt. Recharge by taking siestas, gelato breaks, and after-dark
walks, strolling from one atmospheric
square to another in the refreshing evening air.

red *Pantheon*—which
gest dome until the
rly 2,000 years old
day over 1,500).

of Athens in the *Vat-
odies the humanistic
nce.

gladiators fought
another, entertaining
nce.

is Rome also

Rick Steves books are available from your favorite booksell
Many guides are available as ebooks.

POCKET GUIDES

Compact color guides for shorter trips

SNAPSHOT GUIDES

Focused single-destination coverage

CRUISE PORTS GUIDES

Reference for cruise ports of call

Complete your library with...

TRAVEL SKILLS & CULTURE

Study up on travel skills and gain insight on history and culture

PHRASE BOOKS & DICTIONARIES

PLANNING MAPS

Photo Credits

Avalon Travel
Hachette Book Group
1700 Fourth Street
Berkeley, CA 94710

Printed in Canada by Friesens
Third Edition. First printing January 2021.

ISBN 978-1-64171-323-8

For the latest on Rick's lectures, guidebooks, tours, public radio show, and public television series, contact Rick Steves' Europe, 130 Fourth Avenue North, Edmonds, WA 98020, tel. 425/771-8303, www.ricksteves.com, rick@ricksteves.com.

Rick Steves' Europe
Managing Editor: Jennifer Madison Davis
Assistant Managing Editor: Cathy Lu
Special Publications Manager: Risa Laib
Editors: Glenn Eriksen, Suzanne Kotz, Rosie Leutzinger, Teresa Nemeth, Jessica Shaw, Carrie Shepherd, Meg Sneeringer
Editorial & Production Assistant: Megan Simms
Researchers: Amanda Buttinger, Pål Bjarne Johansen, Robert Wright
Contributor: Gene Openshaw
Graphic Content Director: Sandra Hundacker
Maps & Graphics: David C. Hoerlein, Lauren Mills, Mary Rostad
Digital Asset Coordinator: Orin Dubrow

Avalon Travel
Senior Editor and Series Manager: Madhu Prasher
Associate Managing Editors: Jamie Andrade, Sierra Machado
Proofreader: Rachael Sablik
Indexer: Stephen Callahan
Production & Typesetting: Lisi Baldwin, Rue Flaherty, Ravina Schneider
Cover Design: Kimberly Glyder Design
Maps & Graphics: Kat Bennett, Mike Morgenfeld

Although every effort was made to ensure that the information was correct at the time of going to press, the author and publisher do not assume and hereby disclaim any liability to any party for any loss or damage caused by errors, omissions, jamón addiction, or any potential travel disruption due to labor or financial difficulty, whether such errors or omissions result from negligence, accident, or any other cause.

Let's Keep on Travelin'

Your trip doesn't need to end.

Follow Rick on social media!